Einzelgänger

Unoffendable

The Art of Thriving in a World Full of Jerks

Edited by Fleur Marie Vaz

ISBN: 978-1-70999958-1

Printed by Amazon Kindle Direct Publishing

Second print, January 2021

www.einzelganger.co

Thank you supporters and subscribers.

– Einzelgänger

Contents

Introduction

It's so easy to offend someone these days. Even the act of making this observation can rub a person up the wrong way. Although the internet has made it dramatically easier to trigger people, the inability to cope with mere spoken words isn't a new phenomenon. Human beings have an extensive history of anger, violence and even war because they didn't agree with what other people had to say. Insulting one's religion can lead to mass shootings. Insulting another's mother can lead to murder. Does this mean that we are too thin-skinned? Or have we become more hostile, rude, selfish and disrespectful? I think that there is something to say for both assertions.

Personally, I'd love to see more kindness, compassion and mutual understanding. But as long as there's at least a certain degree of freedom of speech, we cannot stop people from being offended since there's always something that offends someone. This book isn't an attempt to discuss the importance of unpopular opinions and free speech, though. Its cornerstone is the acceptance that the world isn't always nice to us. In fact, the world is full of jerks. What these jerks think and say is *not* within our control. Especially in the current information age that has opened the floodgates of unrestrained expression on the internet, where a-holes in all forms reign supreme.

Stoic philosopher Epictetus observed that, even though the universe is not up to us, our own actions are. While we may not control what nastiness people throw at us, we *do* control how we handle it. When we let our happiness depend on the words of other people, we set ourselves up for a rollercoaster ride without safety brackets. When we hand over our happiness to the whims of others, we'd better be prepared for a tough and painful ride.

The Stoics propose a healthy indifference towards the things we can't control. The less we care about them, the less they harm us. And doing so, saves us more energy to make bold moves that truly matter: we can speak up, disagree, pursue goals, benefit humanity, while being true to ourselves regardless of other people's opinions. Moreover, being *unoffendable* not only means that we don't let the mere words of other humans get to us, it also means that we allow their voices the right to be heard.

Over the years I've gained many philosophical insights that helped me change from someone overly concerned with the opinions of others to someone who cares much less about them. I've learned that the world is filled with people that I don't agree with but deserve as much to be here as I do. I've learned to forge my own path by being less affected by a-holes, bullies and other scum. I've learned that exchanging resentment for compassion helps a great deal in living more peaceably overall. I've learned that there's only one person responsible for my happiness – and that person is me. No one can hurt me unless I let them. I've also learned that the only way to thrive is to ignore the haters and focus on my singular purpose. I've put myself on the path to becoming *unoffendable*.

Wanna join?

A bit about Einzelgänger

Welcome to the magical world of jerk-resistance philosophy! But, before I open the door a little wider, let me tell you a little bit about the person you are dealing with. I will share some of my underlying ideas from my YouTube channel *Einzelgänger* (meaning *Lone Wolf*). So far the guy behind that coffee-brown voice narrating the videos on this channel has been a mystery. So let's first talk about what Einzelgänger is not. I'm neither a psychiatrist nor a psychologist and I definitely don't see myself as some kind of guru, let alone some sage living on a mountain top.

So, who am I? I'm just a guy living an ordinary and modest life, somewhere in the Netherlands. In regards to my credentials, I can say that I have a master's degree in Religious & Ritual Studies and have published several related articles in newspapers and magazines over the years. In the course of my education, I have built a keen interest in philosophy, particularly Stoicism and Eastern philosophy that we can find in Buddhism and Taoism. I've read, listened to and watched tons of it and have experimented with different forms of meditation.

On a personal level, I have gone through several dark 'doomer' phases and existential crises in life as manifested by depression, anxiety, and suicidal thoughts. I've often made a mess of my life. Several key moments that characterized my late twenties and early thirties caused so much pain and confusion that the need to examine my own mind became the last resort to overcome my sufferings. Now, about five years down the road, living more simply and introspectively, I can safely say that I've never felt as peaceful as I do today.

Nevertheless, I make no claims to being an enlightened being dwelling in eternal bliss. I still experience bad days and I haven't tamed all my demons. But I've come a long way from the turbulent times of emotional despair I went through in my teens, twenties and early thirties. It feels like I had been living for so many years in a hurricane and only now has it finally started to subside. Even though this could be because of maturity and changes in life's circumstances, philosophy has helped me tremendously in dissolving the resentment I had towards the world until recently. Sometimes, bits of '*weltschmerz*' come to the surface, but rarely do I attach myself to them as I used to in the past. Accepting that the world isn't fair, that everything changes constantly, and that we're all going to die, really puts things into sober perspective, and helps me to become more grateful for life in general.

I'm still learning, though. I'm still experiencing new things every day. Therefore, I see my work as a testimonial of my own life path thus far, and, hopefully, I'll continue to grow spiritually until I die.

What to expect?

This book is largely autobiographical. Besides presenting a detailed analysis of the nature of insults, it will dive into the workings of the mind, putting wisdom into practice. I'll share my own experiences on how I've become more aware of my own thought processes and emotions to build resilience to the nastiness of other people and acceptance that there are many opinions that I don't agree with.

Wouldn't it be great not to waste so much energy on these things? In the workspace, at school, in public spaces, on the internet and in many other areas of life? Imagine the time and energy you can use for things that truly matter. This book describes philosophical ideas to help the reader gain insight into the 'why,' among other things, the mind works the way it does, and why we shouldn't care too much about what people think and say. I've explained these ideas by using personal anecdotes, characters based on real people in my life, and profound adages from spiritual traditions.

Buddhism, Taoism, and Stoicism are the main sources of inspiration for this book and my YouTube channel. It's no surprise that the schools of this triangle of Indian, Chinese and Greek heritage overlap to a great extent. The Buddha, Lao Tzu as well as the Stoic teachers were all concerned with reducing human suffering; all agreed that human suffering starts in the mind, and that excessive thinking leads to pain.

As Marcus Aurelius famously said: "*The happiness of your life depends upon the quality of your thoughts: therefore, guard accordingly, and take care that you entertain no notions unsuitable to virtue and reasonable nature."*

Chapter 1 – A World Full of Jerks

When the Roman emperor Marcus Aurelius woke up in the morning he would say to himself: "*Today I shall be meeting with interference, ingratitude, insolence, disloyalty, ill-will, and selfishness – all of them due to the offenders' ignorance of what is good or evil.*" This may sound a bit pessimistic, but the notion that we're living in a world full of jerks isn't very far from the truth. When I was young I had difficulty getting my head around this idea. "People shouldn't be jerks," I thought. The problem with this stance is this: if we don't like something, then we'll be unhappy when we encounter it. Since the world is full of jerks anyway, disliking that fact is a sure path to misery.

"..he who fails to obtain the object of his desire is disappointed, and he who incurs the object of his aversion wretched."

~ Epictetus, *Enchiridion*, 2
(translated by Elizabeth Carter, 1758)

Stoicism is a Hellenic philosophy founded by Zeno of Citium in the third century B.C. It is experiencing a revival in our postmodern age. In line with the essence of this philosophy of 'living in harmony with nature,' the Stoics were masters of not taking offense.

Jerks can trigger us in many ways. Someone cuts us off in traffic, a dog owner refuses to clean up the dog's poop, someone at work makes a snide remark about our pink tie. Perhaps someone throws us the f-word or ridicules us at a meeting. "What a jerk!" we think. Jerks come in many forms: your high school bully, boss, neighbor, 'toxic' friends, and even family members who behave in ways that really get in your hair. Yet, according to the Stoics, it's not the events that hurt us; it's our response to those events. So when we're triggered by someone, it's because we allow ourselves to be triggered. We have the freedom to shrug off any disrespect, any insult and ridicule – but of course this is easier said than done.

All the same, I firmly believe that a correct understanding of how things can get to us can lead to overcoming these things. Luckily, philosophers of the past have studied how the mind works, and psychologists have been closely observing human behavior in modern times.

This chapter explores the volatile world of insults. From my experience, insults are the main reason why someone gets offended, even though the 'insulter' isn't always ill-willed or even aware of saying something offensive. The same goes for sharing an opinion that isn't meant to be offensive but is perceived as an insult (or 'hate-speech', which I'll talk about later in the book). So, there is a difference between an insult and taking offense. I outline my philosophical position supported by personal anecdotes and observations. Examining the interesting social dynamics in which insults and taking offense take place, helps us discern between friend and foe in a world dominated by jerks. The list is probably far from complete, so please see it as a humble attempt to create some distinction between different kinds of insults and their nature.

The magical world of insults

Lucius Annaeus Seneca was a Stoic philosopher and also a statesman from the Roman period, who wrote profusely. One of his most notable works is the moral essay *De Constantia Sapientis* (*On The Firmness of the Wise Man*) in which he describes the cool demeanor of the Stoic sage in the face of insults and injuries. A quote that stands out describes how ridiculous it actually is to be offended by an insult:

"If deservedly, it is not an insult, but a judicial sentence; if undeservedly, then he who does injustice ought to blush, not I. And what is this which is called an insult? Someone has made a joke about the baldness of my head, the weakness of my eyes, the thinness of my legs, the shortness of my stature; what insult is there in telling me that which everyone sees?"

~ Lucius Annaeus Seneca,
On The Firmness of the Wise Man, XVI
(translated by Aubrey Stewart, 1900)

The morning as I wrote this chapter I saw a reader's comment on my YouTube channel below a video named *The Power Of Walking Away* that shows footage of me literally 'walking away.' The comment said: "I was triggered by the amount of spread your feet had in your walking posture. That cannot be healthy long term." In the past, I would have been offended by such a personal remark about my body. But, even though this comment invoked some uneasiness, I wasn't offended. I'll tell you why.

Based on Seneca's teaching in *De Constantia Sapientis*, I've created a simple flow chart that I now use as the basis for dealing with an insult. Here it is:

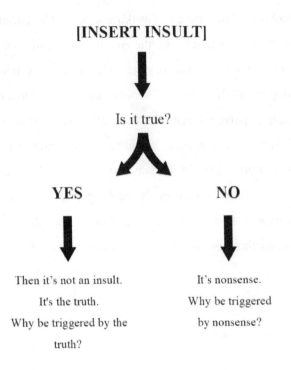

[INSERT INSULT]

Is it true?

YES

Then it's not an insult.
It's the truth.
Why be triggered by the
truth?

NO

It's nonsense.
Why be triggered
by nonsense?

In my case, the 'insult' was the truth. My feet do stand apart more than usual. The interesting part of the comment was: "That cannot be healthy long term." Is that so? I honestly wouldn't know. My reply was: "Would you suggest I have that checked by a doctor then?"

About a week later he replied: "Just walk straighter. It's bad and inefficient, especially if you spread while running. Your gait can become lopsided if you do not control it."

Thus, for what it was worth, my approach generated some advice and my inner peace was preserved.

A simple definition of 'insult' by *Wikipedia* is: *"an expression or statement (or sometimes behavior) which is disrespectful or scornful. Insults may be intentional or accidental."* The problem with insults is that we cannot look into the mind of the insulter. Whether or not I get offended by a comment on YouTube, I don't always know for sure if the comment was meant to cause offense. Sometimes that insult wasn't meant to be one at all.

Insults come in many flavors. Could an 'insult' actually be an invitation to socialize? Perhaps an attempt to have a playful conversation? Or is the insulter indeed a downright, insensitive jerk?

While this chapter aims to qualify the general experience of insults, it is not intended to encourage people to purposefully remain in situations of verbal abuse. On the contrary. Being unoffendable means becoming independent of what people think and say, so we can spend our lives in ways we want to, and connect with the people we choose to, while being able to tolerate the jerks that we inevitably encounter. There's nothing wrong with distancing ourselves from certain people if we have that option. Even if someone has reached the point of being completely unaffected by words (which is great), what's the point really of voluntarily spending time with people that don't respect us and act like a-holes – except, perhaps, we seek some sort of exposure therapy? As Seneca puts it:

"Therefore, although he is self-sufficient, yet he has need of friends. He craves as many friends as possible, not, however, that he may live happily; for he will live happily even without friends."

~ Seneca, IX. *On Philosophy and Friendship*, 15
(translated by Aubrey Stewart, 1900)

The unintended insult

Look, I'm a fairly short guy. Especially living in the Netherlands among the tallest people on the planet, I'm kinda tiny. I remember one day I felt terribly offended by a female coworker who asked me if I didn't have difficulties finding a girlfriend because of my height. Having just broken up after a six-year relationship and feeling terribly insecure about the dating scene, I got literally sick to the stomach by her comment. But her question was sincere. It wasn't meant to be an insult at all. Nevertheless, it still hurt because the question implied that my height makes it difficult for me to find love, which in my state of mind translated into facing a grim "forever alone" future (which isn't the case). Because I took her question as an insult I became resentful towards my coworker even though she bore no ill-will towards me.

Often, unintended insults are more painful for the 'insulter' than the insulted. My brother once made a remark that makes him cringe to this day. In our childhood days, we mostly spent our summers in Spain and stayed at my father's best friend's villa built on a mountain overlooking the Costa Brava. The neighborhood had a private pool and access to a beautiful beach, where you could eat fresh shrimps, squid, 'bocadillos' or enjoy a cold *Estrella* beer while taking in the sea view. A most delightful retreat.

The man – let's call him Peter – was the owner

of a Dutch restaurant in one of the popular seaside resorts. While in his late forties, he got together with a twenty-year-old Dutch woman working for him as a bartender. She migrated from the Netherlands to Spain and moved in with him, exchanging the cold flatlands for this seashore paradise. One day, my brother arrived at the villa after a long journey. Standing in the corridor he yelled: "Well, well! Hasn't she done well for herself, getting together with Peter and now living in a place like this!" Of course, this remark could be taken as an insult to Peter as well as the lady, insinuating that she was a 'gold digger' who found herself a nice catch and that Peter was so foolish to let himself be used by such a woman. What my brother didn't realize was that Peter and his girlfriend were in the room next to the corridor. In the catering industry, staying up throughout the night and sleeping by day is the usual practice.

Despite his youth, my brother already had an exceptionally loud voice, which probably woke up Peter and his girlfriend. He quickly realized that his hosts could interpret his remark as an insult. But, because he was still a thirteen-year-old boy, they probably let it pass (if they had even heard it at all).

24

That's why, when someone insults you, it's always important to realize *who* is doing the insult. Oftentimes the insulter is ignorant, naïve, unthinking, and has no intention at all to offend. Some people are indeed such blabbermouths that they insult one person after the other, and spend a great part of their social interactions apologizing for what they've said. Most of the time, I give these people the benefit of the doubt. But when they are fully aware of their irritating habit but do not address their behavior, now, we are dealing with another creature – the intentional unintentional insulter. In my opinion, these people are just a-holes that are careless about their behavior and, for some reason, refuse to change.

The playful insult

On other occasions an insult *is* meant to be an insult. It is *not* meant to be disrespectful and scornful, *but* is intended to provoke a playful banter. I observe this with male friends all the time: we provoke each other with nasty remarks, insults (sometimes below the belt) simply as a means of social interaction. A playful insult could be your friendly "How're ya doing, asshole?" It could also be like the long 'smear campaigns' in a Facebook group chat I'm in with a couple of friends, towards a redhaired friend of ours we refer to as "the ginger" and often remark he "doesn't have a soul." As you may know, the 'soul' thing has been a running joke on the internet for quite a while, so I guess gingers all over the world have been toughened up by now. My friend has, for sure.

A few years ago I asked him if he ever felt bad about our ginger jokes and he literally said he "couldn't give a shit." Yes, he's become quite unoffendable. Also, he understands the concept of playful insults and knows that we love him no matter what we call him. His ability to be unoffendable is one of the reasons for his successful and ever-growing career as a consultant in a large company. Apparently, he carries that same "couldn't give a shit" attitude in the workplace. This doesn't mean that he is a total jerk, but that he makes a firm distinction between the things that are important and those that are less important. By operating on such a level as a professional the way he does, he simply cannot afford to be triggered all the time by *playful insults.*

Personally, I used to have a hard time understanding the game of playful insults when I was younger. In high school my classmates used to throw these remarks at each other all the time. It was sometimes a bit difficult to distinguish playful insults from true bullying, especially when my classmates directed their insults at me. I absolutely could not handle it. I used to take everything very personally and either got angry or felt intimidated and belittled. Looking back, many of these teasings were actually opportunities for social interaction. If I'd just known that simple truth, my time in high school would have been more fun. I got bullied the moment people started to realize how easily I was triggered. People that are easily incited are the most rewarding targets for bullies because their reactions are pure entertainment. It's fun to poke the bear. Only recently did I begin to realize that not all insults and nicknames (even pejorative ones) are meant to be harmful. In many cases, people start making up nicknames about us and teasing us with insults as playful ways to gain our attention, connect with us and acknowledge our existence.

Years ago I was part of the back office department in the bank I'd worked in for seven years. I consider that particular year as one of the worst times of my life, where I was battling with severe suicidal depression, and an existential crisis followed by a breakup with my girlfriend of two years. Except for my manager, I didn't tell anyone at work about the stuff I was struggling with. One of my coworkers in that department was a woman who created a nickname for me – "Snatsy" – because I had once told a story about trying cocaine in the distant past. In Dutch, snorting cocaine or speed is called "*snatsen*" (a verb). She wasn't familiar with that term and thought it was funny. During the weeks that followed she called me "snatsy." One day, she and a few other colleagues even made a song about me based on *Schnappi das kleine krokodil* (Schnappi the small crocodile), a popular song back in 2004, singing "shni-shna-snatsy snatsy-snatsy-snats." Hilarious! From my utterly depressed state of mind, I thought she hated me. I wondered how she could be such a vixen for creating these silly songs about a coworker. I began to hate her, and started plotting revenge by insulting her back with the nastiest things I could think of (which I never did, by the way).

Surprisingly enough, when she got another job, she told me how much she appreciated me as a colleague and thanked me for "all the fun we had." Fun? Apparently, I often made her laugh, which I didn't realize because of my depression and the conviction that her playful insults and nickname were ill-willed. They weren't. It was her way of connecting with me. People she truly disliked she simply ignored. Ill-willed or not, I can't deny that I found her manner of socializing repulsive and her demeanor arrogant. I suspect she isn't a happy person and I'm glad she isn't my girlfriend.

That said, even though some people have clumsy methods of connecting with others, even the nastiest of insults can be a sign of friendship. A common occurrence not only in my youth but even today, is people calling me "*kleine*" which means "shorty." Oftentimes, this was more of a pet name than a nasty nickname. A pet name could be considered degrading but it isn't necessarily a bad thing. I've got many pet names I use towards friends, which are mostly their real names, changed into more cute cuddable versions. I do this when I sincerely like that person and acknowledge our bond.

However, some people go a step further, throwing us terrible insults and even picking fights to connect with us. I have a friend, let's call him Barry. I met Barry in another section of the bank I used to work. This was more of a side job with a lot of student hires, so the atmosphere was quite casual at times. Barry picked on me to the point that I threatened to kick his ass. The argument escalated quickly until I offered him a cigarette and talked things over together. We became friends after that.

Another example is a female coworker from my last job that took playful insults to the level of utter annoyance. An absolute 'a-holette!' Let's call her Sue. Sue came up with one nickname after another for me and other colleagues. Although my insult resilience had improved, she managed to trigger me big time. I got angry a few times and decided to fight back using a nickname for her. This worked for a while, but she quickly turned it around and began employing different strategies to get under my skin. I've always thought that she hated me, like the snatsy-girl. But when we got closer, I discovered that Sue had a very troubled and traumatic past, which could explain her social lapses. My compassionate self realized that her behavior was her way of showing affection towards the people she liked. We had a lot of conversations about her personal life and, sometimes, I saw glimpses of the real Sue: a vulnerable young woman hiding behind the shield she created to protect herself. This doesn't change the fact that I simply didn't like her behavior and had to call her out a few times. But I do understand a bit better where it was coming from. When I left my job she was the main one who initiated my farewell present.

The 'neg-hit'

A slightly more sophisticated version of the playful-insult can even be used as a seduction technique. The so-called pickup artist (PUA) community (you know, the guys that see picking up women as a sport) calls this a 'neg-hit.' A neg-hit requires skill because it's a remark or question that is not insulting or rude, yet points out the flaws of a woman playfully. This technique is used for seducing women that are high on the totem pole in terms of looks. Most men would put these women on a pedestal and shower them with compliments. A neg-hit, however, is designed to playfully take that woman off that pedestal and align her self-perception with reality: that she is just another human being like the rest of us. According to PUA theory, a man who doesn't treat her as a goddess and doesn't pander to her inflated ego and self-importance, sets himself apart from the majority. This distinction makes him interesting and attractive. He demonstrates high value and subtly lets her know that he doesn't think she's special based on her looks alone, which might challenge her to prove that she, as a person (not as a lust-object) is worthy of his attention. A successful neg-hit highly depends on the situation and how you deliver it.

One of the most hilarious examples I've ever seen in my entire life was performed by my cousin, a seasoned womanizer. We were at a disco-styled *Seventies Party* that took place in our city concert hall. It was very crowded. I stood near the dance floor with a beer in my hand together with a few buddies checking out this blonde beauty in a silver glitter dress. While we were consulting about how we should approach her and desperately looking for eye-contact, my cousin appeared out of nowhere, walked directly towards her and said: "Hey! You must be the disco ball!" The conversation ended quickly, but then, something funny happened: she and her two female friends started following us through the concert hall, clearly showing interest in my cousin. She was probably very aware of her physical assets and that she could get any man she wanted. While men were throwing themselves at her, my cousin stood out. His playful neg-hit demonstrated that he wasn't too impressed, let alone intimidated by her. This caught her interest.

The a-hole compliment

A vicious insult to be aware of is the a-hole compliment. A-hole compliments are insults deliberately disguised as compliments. The reason I think they are so vicious is because the insulter has the clear intention of insulting another person, but is too much of a coward to deliver it directly. So he uses a compliment – with a twist. But it often turns out worse for him. A compliment is meant to show affection towards another person and, when that compliment turns out to be a slap in the face, you breach the trust between yourself and your target. Your target will then be suspicious when you compliment them in the future, and might interpret any well-intended words as a threat. The a-hole compliment is the misuse of virtue to inflict 'a-holeness' on another person, which is a double jerk-action, in my opinion. An example is an overweight person wearing an oversized T-shirt. A normal and well-intended compliment would go like this:

"That's a nice T-shirt."

This compliment is directed at the T-shirt and its function is for the complimenter to express liking for the T-shirt. An a-hole compliment goes like this:

"Nice T-shirt. Covers the rolls pretty well."

This compliment isn't about the T-shirt at all. It's a sneaky way of insinuating that this person is overweight.

When such mixed messages are thrown at me, I always try to see the positive. A good example from my own life is the girlfriend of one of my friends, who typically opens her mouth before thinking. When I met her for the first time I was sitting in a cafe. I had an enjoyable conversation with her and we were both getting a bit tipsy. Maybe an hour later the group decided to leave the cafe to go clubbing. When I stood up, she towered over me. She's quite a tall girl, even by Dutch standards. She seemed a bit surprised by this and commented on it, telling me that I was short. Was this an insult? Nah. I think it was simply an observation. In the club, she didn't hesitate to dance with me. And when we met again a few months later, she made several remarks about my 'handsomeness' (no bragging intended) and that I'm completely "doable despite my height." I could have been offended by that comment, but I didn't, because, although the message carried something that could be perceived as insulting, it was not meant as an insult, just a clumsy compliment.

We can see therefore that an a-hole compliment isn't always intended. In some cases it's an unintended insult couched in a well-intended compliment. As an example, imagine that you're usually not attracted to people of a certain ethnicity, say, Koreans. One day, your best friend comes home from her internship in Seoul with a very handsome Korean young man who happens to be her new boyfriend. Even though you think Koreans, generally, are unattractive people, you think that your friend's new boyfriend is actually pretty handsome. As a matter of fact: he is *hot*. So you say to him:

"You're quite handsome for a Korean."

With this compliment, you say exactly what you mean. You think Koreans are not an attractive bunch, but *he* stands out. Now, this could be interpreted as a compliment and an insult at the same time. But it's definitely a compliment when intended as a compliment. In this case, the main intention is not to point out that *Koreans* are unattractive but that *he* is handsome, even though the complimenter thinks that his group are unattractive most of the time. We can't

36

negotiate personal taste, can we? That's why I don't see any point in getting upset about remarks like these.

Another interesting phenomenon is the way native Dutch people compliment fellow citizens from ethnic minorities. Within their compliment, they often hide a negative message towards the specific group that this person 'belongs to,' which isn't necessarily meant as an insult. This is a classic:

"You are a 'good' one."

This compliment is probably a genuine act of affection towards the receiver. However, the receiver may feel insulted because the compliment implies that the rest of the 'group' are bad news. Another classic:

"Your Dutch is very good for a Turk."

Again, I think that in most cases this compliment is well-meant. However, the Turkish receiver could be offended because this compliment implies that Turks, in general, speak lousy Dutch.

Perhaps the complimenter did indeed, in a viciously subtle manner, want to point out that Turks don't speak Dutch very well. Or the compliment is two-edged, meaning that the complimenter wants to point out that (a) Turkish people in the Netherlands don't speak Dutch very well and (b) that the receiver speaks Dutch exceptionally well compared to other Turks. The main intention of this compliment is acknowledging that the receiver speaks Dutch very well. The receiver may be bothered by the stereotype that the complimenter has of Turkish people in the Netherlands that may not be aligned with reality. How is it possible to make such a judgment without knowing the whole community?

In my own experience, most compliments about language skills directed at immigrants aren't ill-intentioned. But when the compliment is indeed meant to stir the pot, it's definitely an a-hole compliment, thus, an insult. However, if the insult is directed at the Turkish people that lack language skills, why take offense? Remember the flow chart? When it comes to that specific group of Turkish people that indeed don't speak Dutch very well, it's the truth. And if the insult is directed at the Turkish community as a whole, again, why take offense? It's all nonsense. Being offended by nonsense is a waste of time.

The a-hole question

No less double-edged as the a-hole compliment is the a-hole question. An a-hole question is a question that is not intended to be in pursuit of knowledge that the receiver has, but is a way of mocking that person. Initially, you give that person the impression that he or she knows something that you want to know. In this dynamic, most people receiving a question feel complimented. Not only are they being recognized as knowledgeable, but they also have an opportunity to help out a fellow human being. By asking someone an a-hole question you are mocking their knowledgeability and, in their willingness to help you, all they get is a slap in the face. It goes like this:

ME : Can I ask you something important?

TALL PERSON : Of course! What is it?

ME : Well, I was wondering. Is it cold up there? (chuckling)

Some a-hole questions can be very amusing. In my last job, I had a colleague, a middle-aged woman who wasn't the most positive of people. She took great relish in complaining about and deriding colleagues from other departments that (according to her) didn't do their job very well. However, it was the way she complained about basically everything that was absolutely hilarious, especially with her *Cruella DeVil* voice and her strict primary school teacher manner. She, too, became the object of rude banter (mostly behind her back) though she was very aware of that. On top of that, she had a few physical ailments, so the doctor ordered her to perform physical exercises twice a week. With good intentions, I asked her one day if she'd had a nice time at the gym. "Remove the nice," she replied in her Cruella DeVil voice. This cracked me up. "Why?" I asked. And so followed a rant that cracked me up even more. I wasn't laughing at her physical ailments but about the entertaining way she can rant about things in general. She clearly enjoyed doing it, showing a smile like she was chuckling at herself. Although many people would disapprove of laughter incited by other people's misfortune, our conversations at least added a bit of lightheartedness to the workplace.

Since then, I used to ask her the same 'a-hole question' every week – "Did you have a nice time at the gym?" – not only to hear her amusing take but to have an actual conversation with her. Her rants never failed to crack me up and I believe she loved the fact that someone was willing to listen to her. Sounds fair, doesn't it? Yes, and even though it's a bit unconventional, a-hole questions can be great ice breakers, depending on the person. Some people simply respond very well to vicious remarks with a humorous swing. We can try so hard to be saints, but I agree with Alan Watts when he said that a pinch of rascality is part of human nature.

One-hits

One-hits are the complete range of swear words, like 'motherf*****', ***hole, d*ckhead, et cetera. All this is a manifestation of verbal aggression that has one goal: *expressing discontent*. There are exceptions though, which I'll discuss in a moment. I used the name 'one-hits' because insults like these are often simple, spontaneous outbursts, consisting of one or two words at most, that cause a 'hit' on whoever takes offense. Resorting to these types of insults, especially in the heat of debate (which is supposed to be rational) shows weakness. You can't win, your emotions take over, and you start to curse.

One-hits are prevalent in traffic, also known as road rage. This isn't surprising because when you're driving you don't have time to craft well-considered sneers to throw at other road users. Also, the many dangerous situations that occur in traffic often frighten and upset people, creating a spontaneous reaction as swear words. I believe it's a learned practice among Westerners, though. I've spent many months in Indonesia. Traffic in Indonesia is way more chaotic than in, for example, the Netherlands but I've hardly seen road rage. Indonesians seem way more tolerant of the faults of fellow road users, as they probably do the same, too.

I think that most expressions of road rage are the same thing. People might resort to saying things like "f*ck you" or "a-hole;" but that's only because they're startled. I wouldn't take that personally. People do strange things when they're scared. When I was seventeen years old, I was almost hit by a car. The driver hit the brakes just in time. Even though he was in the wrong, he stepped out of the vehicle and starting swearing at me. It was obvious that he wanted to kick my ass. It took only a few seconds for him to realize that I wasn't at fault, so he turned around, stepped into the car and drove away. Aggression was his jerk reaction to the incident. It was the emotion shutting down his rational mind and turning his aggression on me. Again, it wasn't personal.

One-hit insults don't have to be malicious. Heck, they don't even have to be meant as insults, though they can be perceived as insulting nonetheless. They don't have to be profane; regular words will work, too. A friend of mine – let's call him Mark – seems to suffer from a light form of Tourette syndrome in the form of verbal tics. When excited, he blurts out words in an uncontrollable manner. The things that tumble out of his mouth could be names of classmates, family members, the (deceased) leader of Islamic State, a series of diseases, or the expression '*meh*' (an expression of a lack of interest or enthusiasm). When something distresses him, I found out that he's more likely to deliver a one-hit. For example, we're hiking in the forest and suddenly a middle-aged guy on a mountain bike, who's probably in his midlife crisis, cuts us off. Instantly and without any hesitation, Mark screams: *"Abu al-Baghdadi!"* Was this an insult towards the middle-aged mountain-biker? I doubt it. As far as I remember, the mountain-biker was Dutch and clean-shaven. I don't see any connection between Islamic State or Muslim terrorists in general and mountain-biking. In this instance, the one-hit was Mark simply being startled by the biker's sudden appearance. It was an automatic reaction not directed at anyone, and the choice of words was insignificant.

One-hits are also very common among playful insults. Not everyone can appreciate this and I rarely use swear words as one-hits on friends because I think it's going too far. On the other hand, using more neutral terms as one-hits to playfully address our friends in a slightly pejorative manner is fine by me. This takes skill. We not only have to make an estimation if the friend is receptive to this playfulness, we have to select our words carefully as well. Playful one-hits are supposed to be jokes, so they should be funny for both parties.

A former coworker of mine is the master of the friendly one-hit. Let's call him Carl. Carl has the ability to shake funny nicknames out of his sleeve. These nicknames were so effective, they were actually adopted by others and became popular. Carl used completely neutral terms to address people he liked, such as "*tamme herder*" which means "tame shepherd." Him calling people "tame shepherds" was so ridiculous, it was funny, and it became a legendary one-hit on the work floor. Being not-insulting, funny and teasing at the same time was Carl's strength. Unsurprisingly, if Carl is the master of the friendly one-hit, my friend Barry is definitely the king of the unfriendly one. Unlike Carl, Barry wasn't always neutral in his word choices for the one-hits he delivered. Although his *intentions* were often friendly, Barry didn't hesitate to address people as "fool," "idiot" and "dweep." Nevertheless, one-hits were often his unconventional form of socializing, connecting with other people and showing appreciation for them.

To sum up, the insult-grade of one-hits depends on many factors: the situation, the 'insulter,' the way the one-hit is verbalized and, whether the one-hit is consciously executed or not. One-hits could come as an emotional reaction, an uncontrollable Tourette-induced outburst, a demonstration of aggression and dominance, an admission of weakness after losing a debate, or simply a playful gesture to connect with the ones we are fond of. Most of the time, one-hits say more about the person that delivers them than the one who receives them.

Body signal insults

Hands down (pun intended) the most famous body signal insult is showing the middle finger. The value attributed to the middle finger highly depends on the context, the trigger, the person you're dealing with and the facial gestures of that person. The middle finger could be an answer to a playful tease. In this case, the gesture often goes together with a "f*ck you" smile. On other occasions, the middle finger is an expression of anger, which is easily identifiable by a 'not amused' facial expression and, oftentimes, an angry verbal outburst to elucidate the upstanding middle finger. A running joke among friends, and even among my previous co-workers, was the 'subtle middle finger.' This insult (which is a 100% playful in my experience) requires a bit of timing. You either need to predict when your opponent will look in your direction or you need to subtly lure your opponent into looking in your direction. When the timing is right, you'll have your target's eyes falling directly onto your middle finger, which means that your mission is accomplished.

How to perform the subtle middle finger? There are different ways. The easiest and most common way goes as follows. Carefully form a middle finger with the hand of choice. Slowly bring the middle finger towards your face. Pretend that you have an itch on your head. Use the middle finger to scratch the itch, but, do it in slow motion. Make sure that when your opponent looks at you, you turn your face to them and look them directly in the eye with a slight grin on your face. Then you do your thing.

The subtle middle finger is also a great weapon

against an a-hole question. When someone asks you an a-hole question, you simply scratch the side of your head and say: "Good question. Let me think." Body signal insults are often related to culture and I will give a few interesting examples of these later on in the book.

Looking at body signal insults, I think they are harmful to the degree that meaning is attributed to them. If you think that the act of someone giving you the finger is a terrible thing, most certainly you will be hurt. If you don't, you will not. A body signal insult in itself is harmless. I don't think that showing the middle finger has ever physically injured someone. And since this kind of insult involves no words (except, perhaps, f*ck you), what's there to be upset about?

Chapter 2 – Triggered!

Now that we've examined the world of insults, it's time to explore the underlying issue: *Why* are we getting offended? Taking offense means that we are triggered by something or someone. This could be something that we deem insulting. But this could also be an opinion that goes against our own beliefs. At base, being triggered is a form of distress. The Stoics called this *lupē*. Lupē is one of the Stoic passions (*pathos*) which are basically inflictions that people suffer. When we are offended, the emotional suffering that follows is lupē. Some people get triggered much quicker than others, while others aren't triggered at all. No matter what the world throws at them, they won't experience any form of lupē. The reason for these differences is simple. It's not the outside world that offends us but our opinions *about* the outside world. Here is a quote by the ancient Stoic philosopher Epictetus:

"Men are disturbed, not by things, but by the principles and notions which they form concerning things. Death, for

instance, is not terrible, else it would have appeared so to Socrates. But the terror consists in our notion of death that it is terrible."

Epictetus, *Enchiridion*, 5
(translated by Elizabeth Carter, 1758)

Things offend us is because our minds let them. In his correspondence with Serenus, Seneca explained that insult and injury are two different things. When someone throws us an insult, it doesn't mean that we will necessarily be injured. Yet, many are. Moreover, we see that people choose to suffer violence over the injury of insults by getting into physical fights over a few words that have been tossed in their direction. Seneca argues that the inability to endure insults is a form of mental weakness. Please note: at the time Seneca lived, slapping someone in the face with the back of your hand was considered a grave insult.

"If you think fit, my Serenus, let us distinguish between injury and insult. The former is naturally the more grievous, the latter less important, and grievous only to the thin-skinned, since it angers men but does not wound them. Yet

such is the weakness of men's minds, that many think that there is nothing more bitter than insult; thus you will find slaves who prefer to be flogged to being slapped, and who think stripes and death more endurable than insulting words."

~ Lucius Annaeus Seneca,
On The Firmness of the Wise Man, V
(translated by Aubrey Stewart, 1900)

Even though I agree with Seneca that experiencing injury by insult is a sign of a thin skin, I also believe that the way we handle insults is a bit more complicated and well worth reflecting on. The mechanisms that take place in our minds that get us triggered are undoubtedly complex and based on a plethora of life experiences and social conditioning. Culture, religion, intelligence, gender, political climate – the factors that influence our minds to get us triggered are endless. In a highly feminist environment, a woman may be offended by the slightest suspicion of misogyny, and people of ethnic minorities that have faced discrimination will be extra sensitive to what appears to be a racist remark. Then there are socially acceptable behaviors from one society to the next. In

51

the Netherlands, for example, it's very rude to jump the queue. In Southeast Asia, everyone does it. This absolutely annoyed me when I was traveling there for the first time.

Aside from collective ideas of what's tolerable and what isn't, individual experiences play an important role, too, like the way we were treated by our classmates in elementary school or domestic violence in our childhood. As a result of the past, we might suffer from low self-esteem, making us extra vulnerable to insults, which, basically, confirms and strengthens the negative image we have of ourselves. The opposite is also true. When you have an *inflated* self-image, you'll be just as vulnerable to insults as when you have a *low* self-image. This makes me think of a funny story that my father used to tell about two of his childhood friends.

Oh, the fragile self-image...

In their late teens, my father and his friends formed a gang highly endued by the male-dominance instinct that probably began to flourish since puberty. They weren't shy of using bullying and intimidation to assert their dominance in the schoolyard and on the streets, as well as in the bars and discos they visited. Two of his friends, let's call them Bart and Brett, were big and aggressive. A guy had only to look at them the wrong way and they would kick his ass, let alone if some guy would call Brett, Bart or one of their friends "*lul*" (which is the Dutch word for 'dick'). An ass whooper was guaranteed. By comparison, my father – he's of Asian descent for a great part – was short and scrawny. He was reluctant to fight but Brett and Bart were always ready to physically defend him. For his own amusement, he used this fact to pick fights with other guys and let his friends do the dirty work. The only thing he had to do was go to Brett or Bart and say: "See that guy over there? He just called you a dick." How dare they? Didn't they know who they were dealing with? Possibly, the two young men had been delivered a blow to their ego in the past and developed a mechanism to defend it at all costs.

The crucial trigger for taking offense is the perceived attack on one's self-image. Most people are attached to their self-image, which is nothing more than a story to describe themselves and their relationship with the environment. Physical beauty is an interesting phenomenon in regards to self-image. Even though beauty and ugliness may be in the eye of the beholder, there is generally consensus among people about who's ugly and who's beautiful regardless of beauty ideals among different cultures. I believe that the majority of men would agree that Marilyn Monroe was an exceptionally beautiful woman and Lizzie Velasquez isn't. I also believe that the majority of women consider Brad Pitt and George Clooney good looking dudes and Sam Berns less so.

When your physical attractiveness is confirmed over and over by your environment, it becomes part of your self-image. Your looks are now part of the story you tell yourself about yourself. But this doesn't necessarily make this story true. There are people out there that genuinely don't think you're attractive. And, when you are confronted with this undesirable piece of information, your self-image is attacked. This is where the previously discussed 'neg-hit' makes an impact; it rocks the story and creates conflict between ego and reality. Egos are fragile because they need to be fed by the outside world. If they aren't fed, they shrink. If they're threatened, they will defend themselves. A guaranteed way to trigger people that are obsessed with their looks is honest and genuine evidence that they aren't as beautiful as they think. They are offended because their self-image is challenged. You see, some genetically gifted good looking human beings don't just *have* good looks: they *are* their good looks. Thus when their good looks are challenged, their very core is at stake.

The ancient Taoist philosopher Zhuangzi had an interesting take on beauty. He observed that from a human point of view a young woman may be perceived to be beautiful by almost any man. Men throw themselves at her, ask her to marry them, shower her with gifts, which means that her self-image of being a beautiful woman is probably pretty solid. However, we must not forget that her beauty is most likely limited to human perception, because it's only humans that attribute the value of 'beauty' to her. From a wider point of view, she isn't beautiful at all. As an example, humans influence dogs based on scent, mood, and behavior. The dog doesn't care if you look like Jennifer

Lawrence or Danny DeVito. Imagine Jenny taking a walk in the city park on a sunny day. Many men will salivate when she passes by and many women will envy her. But the fish in the pond and the sparrows looking for crumbs in the grass will flee when Jenny comes close. For these animals, she's more frightening than beautiful.

So, for Zhuangzi, instead of thinking, "I'm beautiful," it would be more accurate to think, "Many human beings perceive my past and current looks as beautiful." I say "current" because there's yet another aspect of beauty. Looks fade. The problem with attaching oneself to the story, "I'm beautiful" is that physical beauty is fleeting. Admittingly, some older people are well preserved. But when someone approaches the age of forty or fifty there's a visible decline in looks. Balding, hanging and loose skin, wrinkles, grey hair, pigmentation spots, hair growing out of the ears and generally less energetic radiation characterizes the harsh reality of aging. People who relied on their looks in their younger years now face difficult times because their greatest asset loses value. Some are so attached to their self-image that they are willing to undergo expensive surgery to maintain their looks, and unwilling to accept that physical beauty fades like an apple left to rot.

When you're attached to a certain self-image, whether it's linked to your position in the dominance hierarchy, physical beauty, intelligence, reputation or something else, you're vulnerable to words that refute that self-image. When your story is attacked, you get offended. My former coworker Sue I told you about earlier, once made a remark that gave my self-image a slap in the face. Since the age of seventeen, I've been going to the gym on and off. The fact is that I've built quite some muscle over the years. I went from extremely scrawny to athletic. I'm no bodybuilder by any measure, but most people I encounter notice that I train. So, the story that I tell myself is that I'm quite muscular. Oftentimes I catch myself taking pride in the notion that my body is at least slightly more muscular than average and that the size of my triceps is somehow tied to how attractive I am perceived by the opposite sex. When I've managed to train for weeks in a row and maintain a healthy diet, I feel more attractive than when I've been eating junk and spending the weekends drinking beer and smoking cigarettes. So, when I'm immersed in my training, my muscularity becomes a more dominant aspect of my self-image, which means that I've become increasingly attached to it.

This attachment comes with a dark side. One day at the office I was discussing strength training and healthy food to (in my own words) "maintain my muscles mass while increasing my ability to run long distances." Instantly the sharp-tongued Sue replied: "What muscle mass? Who are you talking about?" Boy, was I offended! For weeks I had been training hard, admiring my progress in the mirror, eating two grams of protein per kilogram of body weight, getting compliments from my peers, and now that woman blatantly denies my physique. I mean: I know I'm not a bodybuilder (not even close) but completely denying my above-average-muscularity deeply conflicted with my self-image.

I never knew the reason that Sue made that remark. But I see three possibilities. Firstly, as the master tormentor she is, she probably knew very well I was attached to my training and saw denying my muscle mass as the ultimate way to rile me. Secondly, her past lovers, male family members, male friends, former male coworkers and other men in her life were all more muscular than me. Thirdly: here's this scrawny dude who thinks he's the cat's whiskers, but really is not. Whatever the reason, it wasn't the remark that hurt. It was my self-image that perceived the remark as a threat.

To paraphrase Epictetus: *we're not disturbed by events but by our opinions about events.* When we look closer at our self-image we discover that it's a story built upon opinion: "I'm beautiful, I'm intelligent, I'm muscular, I'm the alpha male." These assertions are subjective and therefore need validation from other people. This makes them weak and unreliable. External validation is not within our control. Needless to say, the Stoics recommend us not to focus on things beyond our control.

Being offended is conditioned

"...our expressions of politeness, the compliments we make, in particular, the respectful attentions we pay to ladies, are a matter of training; as also our esteem for good birth, rank, titles, and so on."

~ Arthur Schopenhauer, *Studies in Pessimism*

(translated by T. Bailey Saunders, 1891)

When we look at humanity as a whole it is interesting to see that people from different cultures and religions get offended in different ways. An Arab is triggered by different things than a German. A Japanese has a different view of insults than a Kenyan. Like animals, human beings are conditioned largely by their culture. Culture and religion teach people how to think, how to behave towards one another, what things to pursue, desire and what to be averse to. Among these things is the training to take offense in certain things.

A challenge of multiculturalism that I have experienced first hand is that a diversity of cultures means a diversity of propositions towards what's offensive and what's not. This often leads to misunderstandings because someone from a different culture may feel incredibly offended by certain behavior that, in another culture, isn't offensive at all.

A simple and harmless example of this is how we treat food. In Dutch culture, when someone offers us a meal, and we don't want that food because, either, we aren't hungry, or, we don't like the food offered, we not only decline the offer but we state the reason for it – "No thanks. I hate cheese!" for example. However, someone from another culture may see this as too direct or rude. I have traveled to Indonesia seven times. Generally, Indonesians consider it rude when you reject the offering of food. At the same time, I consider forcing someone to eat rude, too.

If you have ever been to the Southeast Asian archipelago you may have noticed that the local people love to take photos with foreigners. Compared to many other cultures, they do not care about privacy that much and often don't mind being photographed or filmed.

One day, a Dutch acquaintance, who was visiting Indonesia for the first time in her life, was approached by an Indonesian woman who politely asked her if she could take a picture together with her. She declined. The Indonesian woman was visibly disappointed and hurt. Personally, I rarely deny these requests because (1) I know that Indonesians are delighted when they manage to be on a photo with a *bule* (Indonesian for 'stranger') and (2) in 99.9% of the cases they are not ill-willed and will not misuse the photos for evil purposes. When my Dutch acquaintance declined the photo request, my first reaction was thinking that this was very rude of her. Later, I realized that I'd gotten so used to Indonesian culture that I would temporarily adapt my behavior to suit their customs. I guess I'm easily trained. When I looked at the situation from a purely Dutch mindset, I could understand why my acquaintance denied the request.

The Dutch value privacy a lot. A stranger asking to do a selfie together is considered very rude unless the person asked is a celebrity. Dutch culture is fairly egalitarian, and the Dutch don't really look up to other peoples (like some Indonesians seem to do) and are used to multiculturalism by now. Asking random strangers to take a picture with them is almost inconceivable. Why would anyone do that? Maybe because of a scam? Thus, I understood her reaction. After I explained to her that some Indonesians are so fascinated by foreign people and that a picture with a foreigner makes them very happy, and that the chance of them using these photos for evil purposes is very small, she started saying "Yes" to these requests.

Arthur Schopenhauer wrote about the

trainability of human beings in his book *Studies in Pessimism*. He stated that the culture in which a person grows up decides what's good and what's bad behavior. He wrote:

"There are many persons who are trained to be strictly honorable in regard to one particular matter, while they have little honor to boast of in anything else. Many a man, for instance, will not steal your money; but he will lay hands on everything of yours that he can enjoy without having to pay for it. A man of business will often deceive you without the slightest scruple, but he will absolutely refuse to commit a theft."

~ Arthur Schopenhauer, *Studies in Pessimism*
(translated by T. Bailey Saunders, 1891)

What Schopenhauer describes we see all the time these days. People abusing their position to indulge in corporate greed are not regarded as criminals per se. But stealing a can of Coca-Cola from the supermarket surely is. Even though many more people are exploited because of the former, the latter is considered worse. We as a society decide what is criminal and what isn't.

Similarly, we as a society decide what is insulting and what isn't.

When I was a kid, I remember that a group of Turkish boys came up to me and a friend once, making these weird hand signals. I wasn't the bravest of kids, so I was definitely intimidated. I was confused as well because of what they did with their hands. One signal was done by turning one hand into the form of a tube by pressing the other fingers except for the thumb against the palm of the hand, while the other hand slapped on the tube hole like those pedal bins opening and closing. The other signal was done by putting the palm of one hand on the upper wrist of the other arm and, then, sliding the upper wrist back and forth, and moving the hand attached to that wrist up and down. As children, we could not comprehend why they were doing this. But later we discovered that these are Turkish insults meaning something like: *"I'm going to kick your ass"* and *"Up yours!"* We burst out laughing because from our Dutch viewpoint this seemed so ridiculous. But for these Turkish boys, it was the conventional way to communicate their dislike of us.

In many cultures, insulting one's mother is a

big thing. In fact, it's one of the worst insults one can ever throw. I tend to see this often in Middle Eastern and North African cultures. My Moroccan Muslim driving instructor once explained to me that in his culture, mothers have an almost divine status because a mother sacrifices so much for her child, from carrying the child in her womb through all the years of sacrifice ahead. Although I generally agree with his vision on mothers, I don't really see why I should go berserk when someone insults my mother. Of course I don't like it if someone bad mouths my mother but I would not get super angry to the point that I would physically harm, let alone, kill that person. This is probably because I wasn't trained to get so heated when someone insults my mother.

Also, I think that *honor* is an important dimension regarding the intolerance of insults. Some cultures are more honor oriented than other cultures and have different views of what's honorable and not. In some Middle Eastern cultures, it is honorable to protect your sister's virginity and, if the wrong person takes her virginity before marriage, avenging this is considered an honorable deed. In a culture steeped in symbolic honor, the retribution of disgrace is a way to maintain a good reputation. This shows that you're able to enforce the values that are present in your community, like the prohibition of intercourse before marriage. If this community perceives insulting one's mother as a serious violation, then avenging someone who does is an act of virtue.

In their book *Culture of Honor, The Psychology Of Violence In The South* experimental researchers Richard Nisbett and Dov Cohen show us that in the Southern states there's a culture of honor among white people. According to their research, U.S. college students from the South are twice as aggressive when they are insulted compared to Northern college students. Also, using violence is considered acceptable in the South as a way to respond to insults, which simultaneously maintains a person's reputation of being strong and powerful. Similarly, a 2016 study named *Honor & War* by Allan Dafoe and Devin Caughey tells us that cultures that place a high value on honor are more likely to go to war: Southern U.S. presidents are twice as likely to use force compared to non-Southern presidents. In ancient history, we can see a good example of honor-induced revenge when Prince Paris of Troy abducted King Menelaus' wife Helen; a deed that resulted in the Trojan wars.

In some Asian cultures losing face means losing honor, which means losing respect, reputation, social standing, and one's very core. Losing face could even be a reason for suicide. Within the Indonesian branch of my family, I still notice the remains of an honor culture. My grandfather, who fought as a child soldier during World War II and got captured by the Japanese, once told me how the Indonesians inflicted the cruelest acts of retribution on all their enemies when the war was over. However, he described with admiration a Japanese general named Yamada, who lived in a mansion in Java during the occupation. My grandfather was forced to work for him as a servant and witnessed the brutal torture of captured American soldiers in the mansion's garden. When the Japanese empire capitulated in 1945, Yamada performed *seppuku* (a traditional form of suicide, also known as *harakiri*) to save his honor. Even though Yamada was the enemy and committed horrible acts of cruelty, my grandfather respects him to this day because of that deed.

Honoring the elderly is an essential part of Indonesian culture, which I've had difficulties with personally. Not that I disrespect older people; but when someone is older than you, this person automatically earns the right to be treated with deference. Culturally, this has some advantages: respect, politeness, kindness, and support for older people. Also, this includes an acknowledgment of an elder's experience, wisdom, and contribution towards the family and society. Within my family, this truly manifests in the way we treat our grandparents. Instead of locking them away in the oblivion of retirement homes (as some Dutch people do), we feel obligated to support them ourselves as much as possible, pay regular visits and really include them in our lives.

But this unconditional respect has a downside. It means that criticizing, challenging and even disobeying an older person – even if this person is wrong or abusive – is highly offensive. In my opinion, 'older' doesn't always equate with 'wiser.' In many cases the younger person is right and the older person is wrong. But, for the elder, acknowledging their wrongdoings or apologizing to someone younger means losing face. This has always been a matter of conflict between my father and myself. No matter how wrong or abusive he is, he always assumes the moral high ground simply because he is my senior. "At the end of the day I'm your father," he used to say.

A more light-hearted (and even funny) example is the Bush shoe incident that happened in 2008 in Iraq. During a press conference, journalist Muntadhar al-Zaidi threw his shoes at the United States President George W. Bush, who ducked and avoided both of them. For a Westerner, the act of throwing shoes is ridiculous. Why should we do that? If we want to hurt someone, using a stick or a baseball bat or our own knuckles would be way more effective. However, in the Arab world shoes are considered very unclean. Throwing a shoe at someone is probably as bad as the vomit-cake that hit Dutch right-wing politician Pim Fortuyn during his campaign in 2002, two months before he was shot and killed.

In the era of globalization, people have become more familiar with exotic insults. This is great because we can take into account what people from other countries are offended by and vice versa. The downside, however, is that life has become more complicated now that we are living in a global village. With more exposure to different religions, cultures, subcultures, opinions, political movements and, in many cases, living alongside them, it has also become more difficult not to offend someone. Does this mean that we should walk on eggshells for each other? Or should *they* become more resilient, and less offendable so *we* can blurt out whatever comes to our head? I think that the answer lies somewhere in the middle. Becoming more resilient ourselves is something we have control over, as well as treating other people with respect and dignity. In this case, our words will do no harm, nor will their words harm us. A classical win-win situation.

The awareness that insults are conditioned can not only help ourselves to understand why we get offended by certain things, it also helps us understand the reactions of other people. We can look at our own reactions mindfully and see if our cultural backgrounds might be inducing them. With me this is certainly the case, since I've noticed that I'm less tolerant towards the younger than the older, which is probably a trait I've inherited from my Asian roots. In other people, we might be able to at least build some understanding and compassion for why they react in ways that might be hard to comprehend at first sight. Funnily enough, this protects us from being offended by someone taking offense.

Chapter 3 – So, You Want to be Liked?

One pronounced human characteristic is this inherent need to be liked by other people. In the tribal age, your life depended on acceptance by the group. In wartime, being part of a group might decide whether you lived or died. In a country like the Netherlands – individualistic and predominantly peaceful since the second world war ended – popularity matters a lot less. I can't deny that being liked by other people has a lot of benefits. Having a social circle can lead to lots of fun, better dating opportunities, and a wide support network.

The Stoics would call having a nice social circle a 'preferred indifferent' (the word 'indifferent' being a noun in this case). According to Stoic philosophy, an 'indifferent' is something we can obtain in the physical world but doesn't necessarily decide our happiness. It's nice to have a good reputation. It's great to be liked and loved by our community and to have many friends. However, without these things a happy life is still possible. Unless you break the law, you won't have to fear for your life if people don't want to hang out with you.

After I obtained a bachelor's degree in 2009 I wasn't able to find a job that would fit with my area of study, so I took a job in a warehouse. This was a wonderful and terrible experience at the same time. The work was horribly boring and consisted mainly of sorting clothing and putting it in boxes. However, some of the people I worked with were fantastic and, in some cases, hilarious.

After several weeks I discovered that the social dynamics among coworkers was complicated. Comparable to prison, there were gangs, rivalries between gangs as well as individuals, and there were prison guards, also known as 'foremen,' each having their own small team. The foremen were often mocked and called 'Nazis' behind their backs. They had their own court circle of so-called 'snitches' that would literally spy on the rest and report back what they had seen. The biggest enemy of the 'snitches' and 'Nazis' was the 'resistance' which could be subdivided into 'active' resistance and 'passive' resistance. If anything, I was part of the passive resistance. I don't like snitches but I don't like wasting energy on fighting them either.

Nevertheless, I sympathized with the resistance because they wanted justice and recognition.

Seeing this social dynamics in play was fantastic entertainment for me as a bystander. To save myself from headache, I never took a firm stance on everything, and was overly agreeable, although I sometimes pushed a few buttons for my own amusement. The Nazis were busy being liked by their superiors, the snitches were busy being liked by the Nazis and the resistance was busy being liked by each other. Away from the battlefield, there were two other groups: the neutrals and the despised. The neutrals were the ghosts: people that don't stand out of the crowd and don't cause trouble either. Neutrals check-in in the morning, do their thing and check-out in the afternoon. One of the neutrals was a woman that absolutely didn't give a damn about anything our co-workers said or did. I respected her because she never allowed herself to get caught up in the drama. She was simply *there* to do her job, collect her paycheck so she could have her beer on a Friday night at the pub.

And, lastly, there were the despised. The despised were an interesting bunch, basically consisting of two people, a man and a woman. I can't remember what they had done exactly but people hated them so much so they were barely talked to on the workfloor. I realized that I would never last in their position. How could you possibly work in an environment where you're despised? The Nazis were hated but they at least had each other and their sense of superiority in the hierarchy, which soothes the pain. I've never been able to see into the minds of the despised, but one thing I know for sure: *they endured*. They endured the coldness, endured the waterfall of jokes, endured the stigma of being 'untouchables.'

I think we can agree that the position of being despised by our fellow human beings is most undesirable. However, the Stoics wouldn't call this a 'vice' but merely a 'dispreferred indifferent.' Yes, these two people were despised by their co-workers. But did that obstruct them from receiving their paycheck? Were their lives threatened? Not at all. We don't *need* other people to like us to survive. Furthermore, the Stoics say that it's better to have a bad reputation and a tranquil mind than a good reputation while plagued by unease. Epictetus said:

"You must watch, you must labor, you must get the better of certain appetites, must quit your acquaintance, be despised by your servant, be laughed at by those you meet; come off worse than others in everything, in magistracies, in honors, in courts of judicature. When you have considered all these things round, approach, if you please; if, by parting with them, you have a mind to purchase equanimity, freedom, and tranquillity."

~ Epictetus, *Enchiridion*, 29
(translated by Elizabeth Carter, 1758)

Do we really need positive strokes from our colleagues, likes on Facebook and Instagram and prestige on LinkedIn by showing off our job titles? As Tyler Durden from *Fight Club* argued: do we really need to work our asses off in jobs we hate, to buy stuff we don't need to impress people we don't like? By yearning to be liked, we want something outside of ourselves. In both cases, we want something that's not up to us. James Frey the author of *A Million Little Pieces* deservedly said: "If you care about what others think of you, then you will always be their slave."

Wanting to be liked can be a rat-race and a terrible waste of time in most cases. Our reputation and the opinions of others are beyond our control. What people think of us isn't our business. Epictetus made a clear distinction between the things that are up to us and the things that are *not* up to us. Things that are up to us are our own actions, like our own opinions, pursuits, desires, aversions. Everything outside our own actions is not up to us. We can influence external things, including other people's opinions about us, but we can never fully control them. Of course, it's smart to impress a potential employer during a job interview. But what that employer thinks about us afterward isn't up to us. At the end of the day, striving for something is always a leap of faith; we control our own pursuits but we don't control the outcome.

On bullying

Closely allied to the desire to be liked is the topic of bullying. For many of us, the formation of our self-image is heavily influenced by traumatic events like bullying. Bullying most likely results in low self-esteem, low self-worth, and difficulty in trusting other people. I've already mentioned that I was bullied in high school for a while, partly because I was so easily triggered. Being raised by a single mother as the oldest child, five years apart from my nearest sibling (my parents divorced when I was a baby), I lived quite a sheltered life during my early years. I never had to stand up for myself within the protective confines of my family.

My mother is a very sweet woman who often soothed and complimented me. My dad, on the other hand, was a strict disciplinarian, who sought to correct my mother's gentleness, by dishing out the opposite treatment in a tyrannical way. This method already implied that there were many things wrong with me. My father was harsh, cold and yelled very often. I feared him and saw the weekends I spent with him as a recurring punishment. Because he was my father, I just obeyed and waited until I could go back to my mother. My dad often told me I was living in 'fairyland' where everything was rainbows and sunshine, when reality is anything but. Living in fairyland is comfortable but it isn't a good preparation for life. When fairyland is your default position, you'll see anything else as a threat. The darker side of life, however, is also part of reality. Denying its existence is a recipe for suffering. When you're raised in a world where everyone is nice and sweet, you're in for a rude awakening once you enter the gates of the real world.

About 2,500 years ago a prince named Siddhartha Gautama was born. He was destined to become either a great king or a spiritual leader. His father the king wanted his son to become his successor, so he steered him towards embracing life as royalty, offering him the best entertainment, the most beautiful women, the most exquisite food in the kingdom. Siddhartha lived for a while in his own fairyland created by his overprotective father, which was full of sensual pleasures that most people can only dream of.

One day when roaming outside the palace walls, he was confronted with the suffering and intransigence of life. From that point, Siddhartha couldn't enjoy luxury anymore. After his son was born, he decided to leave the palace in search of answers to his existential questions. He wanted to break the cycle of death and rebirth. He wanted enlightenment. In his journey, he met with many truth seekers and others who attempted to escape the wheel of suffering. Siddhartha knew that indulgence in sensual pleasures did not help alleviate his suffering, so he tried doing the opposite. He became an ascetic. He slept on beds of needles, ate one grain of rice a day but, when he was nothing more than skin and bones, he realized that self-deprivation did not bring him enlightenment. After he ceased his ascetic practices, he sat under the Bodhi tree where he received enlightenment. Siddhartha Gautama is also known as the Buddha.

Like the Buddha's experience, being confronted with the real world was a shocker for me. I could hardly believe how people, besides my dad, could be so cruel and mean. My biggest step from fairyland into the real world was high school. My early upbringing under my mother's wing had been soft, loving, and organized to be as comfortable as possible. She was a fantastic caregiver and I'm still very grateful for that. My younger siblings posed no threat to me because they were too young and too small. The classy neighborhood where we lived for three years seemed to be modeled after the Godly paradise itself with its beautiful gardens and ponds, children playing, smiling people and happy families. I spent those years at a local primary school packed with these sheltered well-mannered kids. Needless to say, I had a blissful, carefree and, above all, safe childhood.

When I was twelve we moved out of the city into a rural area. My mother made this sudden decision because she found a new boyfriend that happened to live there. We moved in with him and I was sent to the local high school. There I learned how cruel kids can be. It took me a while to realize that high school was not ruled by the law of my mother but the law of the jungle. The law of the jungle is the law of the fittest, and the law of the smartest as a distant second. I was in the fourth grade (fifteen years old at the time) where I got mocked by a few guys that had to repeat that year. They were older and instantly had authority over the younger kids.

A year earlier the law of the jungle had kicked in at home as well. My mother's boyfriend turned out to be an alcoholic, who pointed at my youngest brother as the cause of all trouble, including his relationship with our mother falling apart. Amid the domestic turmoil at my mother's, I began to develop a relationship with my biggest villain: my father. He couldn't stand my mother and made it clear that he wanted me to live with him. Living with this brute had always been out of the question for me. I remember myself screaming at the age of eleven, before we moved out of the city, that I'd rather die than live with my father.

Experiencing serious hardship can radically change your perception of reality. My mother finally got separated from her alcoholic friend and went into deep depression. As a result she had great difficulty running the family as a single mother. Thus, I took the leap of faith and moved in with my father and his partner of fifteen years. I longed for a stable home after such a chaotic period, and that's what I hoped for at my father's. Or so I thought. My father and his partner divorced shortly after I moved in. I didn't want to go back to my mother, so my dad rented a room for me somewhere in the city center.

And so, at fifteen years old, a new chapter began for me. It might have been the inability to cope with these events that made me irritable and unable to handle the insults my classmates were throwing at me. I was an easy target because I showed discomfort by the insults. Also, the way I presented myself attracted ridicule. Visibly depressed by my home life, I walked around like Shaggy from Scooby-Doo with the attitude of an 'emo.' Oh, and I was physically weak and my social skills were poor. I turned inwards for escape. My afternoons and evenings were spent playing video games on my PlayStation and watching porn clips I'd downloaded with a 28.8k modem. I looked a bit like a *doomer* back then, but without the joint, listening to bands like Korn, Limp Bizkit, Rammstein and Slipknot to soothe my pain. Not that this is bad music – but you know what I mean. The difference was that the doomer is existentially driven and I was simply torn by past events.

I remember two guys (who had to repeat that year) sitting right behind me in biology class. Every time I spoke, for example, to answer a question, one of them started provoking me. These weren't even insults, just stupid remarks like: "Oh, well done" or "Good answer" or "You're so smart." I could have laughed with them, gone along with them playfully, ignored them or punched them in the face. Instead, I swiped their study materials from the table on to the floor. This wasn't really effective but I was too scared to punch them. Apparently, my reaction was amusing for the bullies. It showed them I was easy game. When my other classmates found out, I became the further target of ridicule. I'm fortunate that the bullying was only verbal and never physical. Eventually, I started to fight back more effectively, even physically on some occasions. Nonetheless, it left a mark and shaped the way I handled these things later in life.

Now, should I blame myself for the bullying or should I blame the bullies? I blame neither. We often don't know why bullies bully. Perhaps they've been bullied themselves? Or they had a difficult childhood and vent their pain on their victims? Maybe they were ignorant of how they were hurting us. What's happened has happened – we can't change it. As Epictetus said:

"An uninstructed person will lay the fault of his own bad condition upon others. Someone just starting instruction will lay the fault on himself. Some who is perfectly instructed will place blame neither on others nor on himself."

~ Epictetus, *Enchiridion*, 4
(translated by Elizabeth Carter, 1758)

Regretting the fact that you've been bullied in the past won't help one bit. Yes, you could have played it differently and presented yourself differently. Yes, a lot of insults were probably playful and actual invitations for friendship. Yes, things could have been more positive if you did 'this' or acted 'that way.' Beating yourself up about it is just another form of punishment. So is the blame game. Rehearsing the experience in your mind over and over again is simply prolonging the pain. Isn't suffering once from a negative experience enough?

Lose the past, but don't lose the lesson. My past experiences taught me that the way I presented myself attracted bullying, so I started correcting my behavior. Instead of walking like Shaggy, I began to walk straight. By lifting weights, I became strong. By practicing social skills, I was able to make new friends. By becoming more aware, I could detect early stages of potential bullying and nip them in the bud. But the final effort was becoming less offendable and overall a more easy going person that was fun to hang out with.

And, even though I advocate letting go of past events, there are different ways to deal with past bullying. David Goggins offers quite an unconventional approach to this. Goggins is regarded as the toughest man alive. He is a retired US Navy SEAL, a former United States Air Force Tactical Air Control Party member who served in the War in Afghanistan and the Iraq War. On top of that he is the former world record holder for the most push-ups done in 24 hours, an ultramarathon runner, triathlete and ultra-distance cyclist. In his youth he was severely bullied and called the 'n-word' every day, being one of the five Afro-American kids in the entire high school. He was a weak kid who ran away from everything challenging.

This habit continued well into his thirties until he'd had enough after he came home from work spraying for cockroaches. He had no self-esteem, no self-worth, was overweight, and he was done with that. He began to build himself up to the man he is now. He took all the bullying and humiliation and used it as fuel for his great accomplishments. So, instead of attaching himself to his negative experiences and moaning about them, he used them as fertilizer for life. He admitted that for doing this he had to develop a mindset of becoming impervious to any insult. This meant that, even though he had been hurt in the past by all those nasty things people said to him and the frequent beatings he endured, he simply had to start not giving a f*ck about what other people said. He had placed way too much value on the opinions of others. In an interview on the Joe Rogan podcast, he describes his former self as a clown whose life revolved around impressing some people and making other people laugh:

*"I would sit at home, and instead of studying, I would think about: what can I do to impress the motherf*ckers at school. That became my life."*

~ David Goggins, *Joe Rogan Experience* #1212

Later on, he came to understand that focusing your attention on being liked by others is a dead-end alley. Instead he delved deep into the darkness of his soul, harvested the power he found there and turned that into extraordinary accomplishments. Without a doubt, this is much better than letting the past eat you up on the inside.

After I graduated from high school, I was hypersensitive to anyone I suspected would pick on me. Making friends wasn't the problem but keeping them was. I always thought they were snitching on me behind my back. Playful insults still worked the hell out of me. I didn't think of them as playful at all, but as another way to attack me and take me down. I had two extremes. The first was hostility. The second was validation seeking. My social interactions almost always started with the second extreme. Like David Goggins, I wanted people to like me because, when people liked me, they wouldn't bully me. Deep within, I wanted to prevent what had happened in high school. Unfortunately, this worked against me many times. At the end of the day, no matter how well you play your cards, you can't prevent people from bullying you. If they will, they will.

At base, what other people think about us or how they view us is simply none of our business. And realizing that the opinions of other people are none of our business is a very liberating thought. It doesn't only mean that we have no business being in the minds of other people, it also means that there's no reason to be affected by what other people think about us. Isn't that great? Let's take my YouTube channel as an example. I admit that I delete comments sometimes. There are comments with rude language (including the f-word, for example) directed at myself or others. I delete these comments because I think they don't belong on my channel, don't add anything useful to the discussion or add anything of value to other people's lives. They just ruin the atmosphere and therefore I don't want them in my comments section. However, I am rarely personally offended by these comments, partly because I don't take seriously anyone who anonymously insults people on the internet, and partly because I am not responsible for their opinions.

I should add that caring less about the opinions of others doesn't mean being a pushover. If bullying becomes severe and even physical, it surpasses the realm of simply 'offending.' My experiences at high school taught me how to recognize the first signs of bullying. When I notice these signs I realize that I have choices. I can choose to *truly* not care about it (which is difficult, I know) or address it to prevent further escalation. Whether or not someone crosses this line, really depends on the specific situation, so I can't say much more of use about that. But, if I conclude that someone systematically obstructs me in my daily life, then I will either muster the courage to deal with that person, or walk away, in both cases with the intention of self-preservation.

When standing up for yourself, being unoffendable helps to deal with the possible shame and ridicule that often follows. The fear of shame and ridicule is often the reason that people don't confront a bully or decide to forsake the snake pit. However, forsaking the snake pit isn't always necessary. Imagine that you have a job you really like but a coworker keeps harassing you. In this case, I think that the best way is confronting the person, so you don't give a jerk the power to drive you away. This doesn't have to include resentment, shame or other negative emotions at all.

I've been closely observing the two dogs of my parents lately. One is the mother and the other is the daughter. Because the daughter is at the puberty stage, she is hyperactive and reacts to everything that moves.

She often challenges the mother to play with her by biting her neck or legs. What strikes me is that the mother really doesn't give a damn about what the daughter does – until she crosses a line. When that happens she corrects her. After that, they both continue their lives as if nothing happened. When it comes to bullying and harassment, I think we can learn a thing or two from dogs.

I remember during my first year in college how hard I tried to fit in with the cool guys; but it never really worked. I think that the people that I tried to impress saw through my facade and knew that I wasn't being authentic. I even resorted to bullying (the very thing that I despised) to gain popularity. This often backfired because I chose the wrong targets. It reminded me, though, that I'm perfectly able to be a monster myself. If people have a dark side, it's not surprising that I have one, too.

Life has taught me that jerks are everywhere and bullying doesn't stop after high school. People can be incredibly cruel, and often for no reason that we can control. A world full of jerks is just one of those harsh realities of life. We can do everything right and people still may not like us and behave like a-holes. Why make our happiness dependent on such unreliable factors? Why let the bullies decide how we feel, even many years after?

Chapter 4 – Inner Work

"One should give up anger, renounce pride and overcome all fetters. Suffering never befalls him who clings not to mind and body and is detached."

~ The Buddha, *Dhammapada*, 221
(translated by Acharya Buddharakkhita, 1985)

In the previous chapters we agreed that no one, other than ourselves, is responsible for our own feelings. Good emotional and cognitive hygiene means that we have to take responsibility for our own faculties. Nevertheless, we humans are very prone to blame others for our negative mental states.

As you may know, the Netherlands is a bicycle country. Unfortunately, bicycle theft is very common. At one point, I lost three bicycles in one year because of theft. Every time this happened I became very angry, which I took out on my then girlfriend. Righteous indignation came upon me. The problem with anger, however, is the damage all round it causes. It didn't make sense to swear at my girlfriend or punch a hole in the door because my bicycle was stolen, right? Although I don't believe I've ever punched a hole in the door, I did dump on an innocent girl in a way that distressed her. Anger is contagious and damaging. It's a true energy drainer. That's why I've slowly turned my back on the popular notion that we should let anger out. The collateral damage isn't worth it. Because of its destructive nature, there is no righteous anger. Is there something as righteous cancer?

When I gave in to anger, I handed over my power to someone I'd never even met: the bicycle thief. This thief may have been responsible for stealing my property but is this person also responsible for my state of mind? Of course not! In the same way that the opinions of others are none of my business, my mental state is none of his. How I react to having my bicycle stolen is completely up to me. The world isn't responsible for how I feel: I am. Embracing this is crucial to becoming unoffendable.

Keeping our faculty in order

When we suffer because people's opinions and

worldviews aren't aligned with ours, we tend to extend our energies outside of ourselves. Some people expend a tremendous amount of energy in trying to change other people's minds. I don't think that there is anything wrong with trying to influence fellow humans for the sake of justice or out of a sense of goodness. However, I don't think that we should place such pursuits above our primary responsibility which is to keep our own faculty in order. This is a reliable and worthwhile pursuit because we are the masters of our own mental states, not those of others. Have you ever encountered those people to whom you give the same advice over and over again, and they still persist in the same behavior? They never seem to learn. It's a frustrating and time-consuming exercise that rarely pays off.

Hate speech

On this subject, let's talk a bit more about my friend Barry. Even though he loves insulting other people, he has a low tolerance for insults directed at him, especially when he is drunk. When we both studied at the same university we went out all the time and regularly got into conflicts because Barry felt offended by someone. He somehow always needed an antagonist to direct his rage at when drunk.

Why give other people the power to spoil our evening entertainment? Nightlife is often rough, chaotic and not without disturbances because most people are, temporarily, much braver than usual after a few glasses of liquid courage, and are less likely to restrain themselves verbally as well as physically. An overly bold guy may bump into you or throw you an insult or hit on your girlfriend; these things are to be expected at night clubs. A good meditation before going out would be a slightly altered quote by Marcus Aurelius, which goes like this:

"Begin each night out by telling yourself: tonight I shall be meeting with interference, impoliteness, insolence, rudeness, ill-will, and impertinence – all of them due to the offenders' unconsciousness by intoxicants."

Being unoffendable is a form of freedom.

Specifically, we are free from other people's power over us because we couldn't care less about their nasty remarks. This might seem a small thing, but how many have been killed and how many wars have been fought because people were unable to stomach the words of a fellow human being?

If we humans were just a little less offended by other people's opinions, the world would be such a better place. Wasn't Adolf Hitler, in essence, severely insulted because he wasn't accepted into art school, which only fueled his hatred towards the Jews? The day I'm writing this, a man named Kane Burns is jailed for ten-and-a-half years for killing his friend and burning his body because he insulted Kane's mother. And let's not forget that Dutch film director Theo van Gogh was literally slaughtered because his work insulted Muslims, and that the Charlie Hebdo attacks happened because the shooters felt offended by cartoons that criticize Islam.

Today's religious extremists are truly the antithesis of the unoffendables. Isn't it insane to kill other people because you don't like their opinions, even if they're about your religious beliefs? Apparently, many are willing to do so.

Even though, as I stated in the introduction, this book isn't an attempt to discuss the importance of freedom of speech and unpopular opinions, there are a few things I want to address to support my convictions. The purpose of free speech is to share our opinions without being censored or penalized, and I'm happy we can do that in most countries. However, some people see this right as license to shoot their mouths off at anything and anyone, and expect to get away with it. They are oblivious to the reactions of those that feel offended and abused.

As a result many people had rather see hateful speech disappear. But is that really the solution? The question I have in regards to prohibiting so-called 'hate speech' is this: who defines hate speech? By saying that pets can be a nuisance and should be banned from public parks, I might anger the animal rights society because my speech is derogatory and offensive. Should I be punished for voicing an unpopular opinion? Should one be silenced when mere criticism happens to offend someone?

On America's college campuses, students like

to complain about the many things that offend them. Southern Methodist University removed the 9/11 memorials because they might be considered "triggering, harmful or harassing." And the University of Wisconsin issued an "inclusive-language guide" to help staff and students avoid words that might offend someone. Among these words are "ugly," "illegal alien" and even "you guys" (to point to a certain group like Latinos, Afro-Americans, Asians, et cetera). The term 'homosexual' is seen as an offensive reference to gay or lesbian people at Emerson College.

And, in contribution to world peace, the UN has published a comprehensive set of language guidelines under the banner of 'inclusiveness.' Among the words expunged from the language are gender specific terms like 'manpower,' 'mankind,' 'mail man' and replaced by more inclusive, anemic language like 'human power,' 'chairperson,' or, worse still, 'chair,' and 'postal worker.' Talk of political correctness!

Policing the language has become an obsession among many 'progressives' in our society. I was baffled when a British GP was fired for addressing a bearded patient wearing a dress as "Sir" when 'she' had registered 'herself' as female! Is language in danger of losing its color and stripping us of our right to define reality the way it is, one asks?

This argument was raised years ago by George Orwell, who rightly expressed concern about the deterioration of our culture and society alongside the deterioration of our language:

"Now, it is clear that the decline of a language must ultimately have political and economic causes: it is not due simply to the bad influence of this or that individual writer...It becomes ugly and inaccurate because our thoughts are foolish, but the slovenliness of our language makes it easier for us to have foolish thoughts."

~ George Orwell,
Politics and the English Language, 1946

My question is: do all these measures to police the language really solve the real issues – intolerance, entitlement and hate?

What characterizes the measures I just described is the sole focus on the outside world with no regard for the inner world. Being offended by an insult

100

involves at least two parties: the 'offender' and the 'offended.' The 'offender' doesn't always intend to be offensive. Saying "you guys" to a group of, let's say, Dutch, might just be directed at the Dutch in general or in a certain context, for example, "You guys make the best cheese!" We can view this either as a compliment or an offense because it generalizes Dutch people and we don't like that. In this case, the insult is defined by the insulted.

The insulted may also have decided that certain terms are insulting and their goal is to prohibit such terms so they (and others of the same ilk) won't be insulted anymore. Simply put, they want to alter the world to their own liking, including people's speech, thoughts and behavior. We can't be surprised that such demands evoke resistance. Clearly, the world doesn't want to be changed. We cannot force people to dance to our tunes. That's why it's important to accept that trolls will be trolls, that trolls are beyond your control. God forbid, we ourselves might be the trolls! The other extreme in this situation is the act of systemically treating others with disrespect, simply because the law allows us to. Or, in other words, being the proverbial a-hole because freedom of speech entitles one to do so.

Honestly, I'd love to see a nicer, more inclusive and more respectful society. But I know that there will always be jerks. And I also know that most people will not be unoffendable and, thus, will be outraged, hurt and insulted from time to time. No matter what side we're on, in both instances what happens is not up to us. Blaming the other party for getting offended and, for example, 'being a pussy,' is just as tactless as demanding the world to be completely stripped of offense. Although being unoffendable means becoming more resilient to what other people say, we're still humans with flaws and weaknesses. Thus, the mindset of unoffendable always includes a sense of compassion. The 'philosopher' described by the Stoics is an *ideal image*. So is the '*arahant*' described by the Buddhists. I think it's great to strive for an ideal, without forgetting our shared humanity. We can't demand perfection from our fellow human beings, especially when we aren't perfect ourselves.

Once I made a video about conscientiousness. I started the video with a joke about not having a dishwasher or a girlfriend and that I'm not living with my mother either. Afterwards, I was agitated because some viewers saw this remark as sexist. Even though I can 100% guarantee that there were no sexist intentions behind that joke, some people still argued it was a sexist joke. This was very frustrating so I lashed out at one of them, saying:

"Just to be clear: it's a joke. And it's not sexist at all. It's actually self-deprecating humor in regards to my laziness. BUT... If you're so eager to interpret it as sexist, that's fine and your choice. Not mine."

I don't regret my reaction, although I wondered afterwards why I was so agitated by this accusation. I don't know the person that accused me. I don't know if it's a troll, a 'social justice warrior,' or someone that has truly suffered bad experiences because of sexism. If I'd been a bit more compassionate, my reaction would have probably been different. On the other hand, the one that accused me of sexism shouldn't have judged me so quickly, in my opinion.

On another occasion, a young Jewish woman

sent me a message related to a video that portrays the image of a greedy man with a big nose. She told me that the image is a stereotype of a typical 'greedy Jew' and asked me why I used it. She pointed out her concerns because she enjoyed my videos and wanted to be sure that I'm not an antisemite. Because she carefully explained what bothered her, I wasn't offended at all. Instead, I felt compassion and sent her back a message explaining that I wasn't aware of the Jewish allusion and that I'm definitely not anti-semitic. So, it's not just the 'what;' it's the 'how.'

What's my solution? You've guessed. My solution is getting that place between our ears in order and becoming as unoffendable as possible. Why? Because this is the only thing that we fully control. Ancient wisdom from Buddhism, Stoicism, and even Taoism can help us in this process, along with desensitization by practice and exposure.

Focusing on doing our own mental housekeeping also allows us to become overall more loving, useful and respectful members of society. I think I can safely say that the wisdom of old weighs heavily against the current trend of taking offense at everything as well as being extremely reactive towards any insult thrown in our direction. That said, I do believe that even the ancients already noticed that humans in general don't have thick skins. As Seneca wrote:

"..many think that there is nothing more bitter than insult; thus you will find slaves who prefer to be flogged to being slapped, and who think stripes and death more endurable than insulting words."

~ Lucius Annaeus Seneca,
On The Firmness of the Wise Man, V
(translated by Aubrey Stewart, 1900)

Call me an idealist, but if schools would teach children that they're responsible for their own mental faculties and that the opinions of others are none of their business, many problems would be solved. Being unoffendable isn't just about resilience to offensive language; it's also the acceptance of unpopular opinions and the acknowledgment that our fellow human beings have the right to speak, regardless of what we think about it. Roman emperor and Stoic philosopher Marcus Aurelius had to deal with many difficult people throughout his life. He concluded that when someone acts towards him in a nasty way, it's "due to the offender's ignorance of what is good or evil." Instead of pointing out other people's flaws, I think it's a much better investment of our time and energy to actually be the change we want to see.

Coping with bigotry

I'm half-Dutch. The other half is a mixture of Indonesian, Scottish, Italian, Jewish, and possibly even more ethnicities than I'm aware of. The gods decided to bless me with Middle Eastern looks. Having Middle Eastern looks in the Netherlands has its minor disadvantages. It's yet another reason to get picked on and excluded by the kids in the countryside. In supermarkets, the security guards would coincidentally walk through the same corridors as me. Sometimes, I see people getting a bit nervous when I enter a train or bus. When I went out to bars the bouncers would deny me entrance because I wore the "wrong shoes" or because I had been "fighting" last week (even if I wasn't even there). Even my own family members have made jokes about my appearance.

During my first year in college, I met a Moroccan guy who became a great friend and still is today. Let's call him Hamid. I remember that I added Hamid to MSN shortly after meeting him (which was the thing back then) and during the night when I was browsing on the internet, he popped up on my friend's list with the status 'online.' His username was (yes, in capital letters):

"FIGHT AGAINST RACISM AND FASCISM!"

This in-your-face MSN-name was decorated by a series of emoticons – I forget which. Being fed up at the time with people treating me like crap because of my appearance, I instantly liked him. As our friendship grew, we exchanged a lot of experiences about racism, prejudices and our lives as ethnic minorities in the Netherlands. We both had a keen interest in politics and a range of intellectual subjects. Hamid seemed very sensitive to other people's opinions about him and his ethnic group. I remember him arguing with an old lady who seemingly mumbled something denigrating towards us, while we were walking in front of her in a busy shopping street. It was clear to me that Hamid was jaded by past experiences and decided to fight anyone who tried to insult or humiliate him. Sounds fair, right? I think all that Hamid wanted was justice. I understood him completely. Some people can be immensely racist. I've experienced this first hand. Growing up in a country that's supposed to be your home where you want to feel accepted and liked, and you're treated like subhuman scum instead can be very painful. Other kids' opinions of us do matter a lot, especially because society does not teach us to be indifferent to what other kids think about us.

Other kids not liking me because of my ethnic background wasn't a pleasant experience. But I understand now that most kids are simply ignorant. They often can't separate right from wrong and are blind to the damage they inflict on others, or fail to care. I remember when living in the countryside, a village girl didn't want to shake my hand when I introduced myself to her. She looked at me as if she saw a cockroach – pure disgust. Incidents like these have left quite a mark.

After Hamid finished college he started his career. Sometimes he told me about racist incidents at work. I always listened to his story and nodded, sharing my disapproval with him. "It's so unfair," I thought. "He's working so hard and he's such a nice and smart guy. Why does he need to go through this because of a bunch of bigots?" Well, later on, both of us started to realize that the world is indeed unfair. And there's nothing we can do about it. In recent years, Hamid excelled not only in his career but also in finally letting go of his energy-draining "fight against racism and fascism" anger. He discovered that the way to succeed as a person from an ethnic minority is to cast off the victim mentality and start caring less about the haters.

Even though this book is about building resilience and becoming unoffendable, I do not condone jerk behavior. I hold decency in high regard. Being unoffendable is a tool; whether it's something good or bad depends on what the owner does with it. I do think we are responsible for our own feelings but I do not advocate using that as a reason for being an a-hole to everyone and ridiculing anyone who gets upset. When I insult a group of Hell's Angels, I shouldn't be surprised if they kick my ass, even if I think that insults should not be answered with violence. People are people and the majority of them will never reach the enlightened realm of the unoffendables. The majority are very thin-skinned. Thus, I also strongly believe that having an unoffendable faculty ourselves comes with the responsibility to use it virtuously and not as empowerment for our inner a-holeness. After all: we don't benefit humanity by deliberately offending Muslims, Jews, or straight white males, or someone's mother for the sole reason of offending them, now do we?

Chapter 5 – The Power of Indifference

The word 'indifference' has a negative charge in our society. When I hear this word I think about someone shrugging their shoulders as a response to everything that happens. Even when injustice is played out before that person's eyes, he or she just looks away and moves on. Or when someone shows kindness to that person, he or she answers with a toss of the head which says, "I don't care."

The Stoics have a term for indifference – apathy. But to them, apathy has a different and more positive meaning than we do. The Greek word '*apatheia*' points to a state of mind in which one experiences a rational and non-emotional response to the things that are not in our control. This state of indifference towards externals leads to freedom of passion. Apatheia is one of the conditions to reach a state of '*eudaimonia*,' which is the human experience of flourishing and happiness.

I'd like to start this chapter with a story about my friend Mark. I told you about him before; he has, so it seems, a mild form of Tourette, which makes him blurt out words in an uncontrollable manner sometimes. What characterizes Mark is that he can be ridiculously and almost painfully Stoic in regards to insults. In the previous section, I've shown an example of a man who murdered his best friend because he insulted his mother. It isn't uncommon for people to get heated when someone insults their mother. Furthermore, some cultures train people to think that insulting someone's mother is the worst thing one can do.

One day, Mark told me that he simply doesn't understand all the fuss about insulting one's mother. "Who cares?" he said. Sadly enough, his mother had passed away not long before he made that statement. He continued by saying: "When someone tells me that my mother is a whore, I just tell them, "No, that's not possible because my mother is dead." Now, that's Stoic. His position may seem incredibly cold and indifferent and for a great part, this is true. Knowing him quite well I'm certain, that he is neither cold nor indifferent towards his mother's death at all. This doesn't mean though that he should be offended when other people (especially people he doesn't know)

112

badmouth his mother.

Let's get into this a bit deeper. When we are affected by someone insulting our mother, it's because our ego (the story we tell ourselves) is attacked. Because we are attached to our mother, we love her, we don't want any harm to come to her. Therefore, we might feel protective of her. Because we love and respect our mother, we demand that other people respect her, too. When they don't, they attack our story about how the world should be. We are attached to our narrative, so we feel threatened when it's attacked. But consider this: attaching ourselves to stories about how the world should be (and how people should behave towards us) will only lead to suffering because the world is completely out of control. Insults can only harm us when we strongly feel that our reputation is at stake.

I won't deny that a good reputation is a great asset. A good reputation can open many doors for us when it comes to careers and relationships. It draws people towards us and creates the opportunity to help others and be helped. But, according to the Stoics, this is only a 'preferred indifferent.' The problem is that indifferents are still unreliable and so they shouldn't be our main focus. Even though we are looked up to by millions of people, this is no guarantee of happiness. Just look at the many celebrities that died because of a drug overdose and suicide. Robin Williams was rich, famous, talented, successful and liked by many. How could such a person commit suicide? His act shows us that preferable external things like money, fame and material success do not necessarily make us happy. In the same way, unpreferable external things like physical unattractiveness and a bad reputation do not necessarily make us unhappy, either. At most, external things bring us a superficial sense of happiness that is as volatile as, let's say, the cryptocurrency market.

Many people have complimented me on my YouTube videos. I could start telling myself the story that I'm a popular YouTuber and attach myself to that story. I feel great as long as I'm popular. But when my popularity wanes, I lose the story I'm attached to, so I feel miserable. The problem here is that my popularity is not up to me, because popularity is based on the opinions of other people and could be fleeting. And so it is with insults. If insults disturb us, we are still attached to the opinions of others.

If we want to develop a healthy relationship with the world around us, developing a healthy form of indifference might just be what we're looking for. Indifference can be a power. Or even better: a way to prevent giving our power away. When Mark is indifferent to someone insulting his mother, he doesn't give away his power to those that insult her. Getting triggered by the words of another person is giving away your power because you allow them to get a reaction from you. Therefore, we could say that bullying is power play. When the bully succeeds in getting a reaction from a target, they succeed in exerting power over that target. The bully has the power to control the reactions and mental state of the target to some extent. The target may become angry, cry or hide. Whatever the reaction is, it's a consequence of how the target positions itself towards the bully and is not a function of the bully itself. A trained person with a strong mental state can simply ignore the bully and even be genuinely unaffected by any insults from the bully. Or they can even react calmly and kindly in a way that completely disarms the bully.

Healthy detachment

I've already argued that the word 'indifference' may be a bit unfortunate. Even though the Stoic version of indifference aligns with their ideas of virtue, I don't think it's easy to sell indifference, since it can come off as uncaring, avoidance-seeking, even aversion. This doesn't really sound like a fun place to be in. A term that's more appropriate to describe this Stoic mindstate of being free from passions caused by external things is 'healthy detachment.' But, how do we decide what's healthy and what's unhealthy detachment?

Let's do some reverse thinking here. Unhealthy detachment lies in the domain of nihilism. It's the complete disinterest in life and the universe. If you're detached to such a degree that you don't care about anything in the world anymore, you may as well jump from the Golden Gate Bridge – don't! There's no point in living when one's completely apathetic towards life.

Now, healthy detachment means that we are still very much involved in the world, but don't cling to its treasures. Healthy detachment means that we can own stuff but that stuff doesn't own us. For instance, the things I own are purely functional: a TV, a laptop, a computer, a camera, a bicycle, clothing, shoes, and basic furniture. I'm not emotionally attached to any of these things. If the apartment I rent were to burn down, I wouldn't really care that much. I'd probably get some money from the insurance company to buy new stuff. Besides the inconvenience, life goes on.

The Buddhists concern themselves a lot with detachment. According to them, clinging and cravings (forms of attachment) are the very root of suffering. Take romantic relationships, for example. In today's world, love is often mistaken for romantic love. But in most cases (if not all) romantic love isn't loving at all. It's an attachment. It's lust. It's a craving. How can we call something love if it has the propensity to switch from intense affection to intense hate all in one day? We can't. True love always goes hand-in-hand with detachment. Genuinely loving another person is making that person feel free.

Clinging is the opposite of detachment. The problem with clinging is the denial of impermanence. Everything is in a state of flux. People and objects come and go, ideas and opinions change, the past is already gone and the future is uncertain. If we cling to any of these things, we want something that's already gone or hasn't yet arrived. Wouldn't it be better to detach ourselves from living in such a way that we are engaged, yet not bothered, by the ever-changing state of nature? When everything other than our own actions is beyond our control anyway, then why attach to it?

Healthy detachment means that we do allow ourselves to care, and do allow ourselves to give a damn about what's happening in politics or with our loved ones. But, at the same time, we do not *attach* to the world and aren't really bothered when the results do not match our preferences.

A Stoic exercise that helps with this healthy detachment is embracing whatever the outcome is. The German philosopher Nietzsche called this attitude *amor fati*, which is Latin for 'love of fate.' Amor fati doesn't mean that we should just sit there and let the world go by completely indifferent to what happens. It's still perfectly fine to have goals and to work on something great. However, this doesn't mean that we have to attach ourselves to the outcome all the time. The outcome lies somewhere in the future and, most likely, doesn't depend on your actions alone. There are many factors at play that can influence the outcome; many of these factors are not up to you.

For most of us, it's a bit strange to detach from the results when we are working on something. Needless to say: our society is extremely results-oriented. The problem is that, by attaching to results, we get ourselves stuck in the future. This denies us the full experience of the present moment. However, if we let go of the future, we regain our focus on the present moment, which will only increase our productivity. *Now* is the place where the future is made. By detaching ourselves from the outcome, we become more relaxed. We worry less. Why should we be bothered by anything when we do not embrace the outcome anyway?

I see that the people that are extremely prone to being affected by what jerks say are also the ones that have difficulty in detaching. They might hold on to the future, to the past, to the story they tell about themselves, to the opinions of others, et cetera. I remember that a few years ago I was discussing with a friend several frustrations I had regarding my Middle

Eastern looks that do not accurately represent my true genetic background. Looks are everything in this world. No matter if you're Asian, Dutch or from planet Mars, if you look like, let's say, a Turk, people will regard you (and treat you) as a Turk. So when I meet new people I always seem to create great confusion, simply because I look a certain way.

"Well," my friend said before he took a sip of his beer, "You just have a bit of an unfavorable appearance."

I remember laughing off his remark that night. But the weeks that followed, his comment kept nagging me. It evoked all kinds of questions and insecurities. "Will I be forever cursed because of my looks? Is this the reason why people have treated me badly in the past? Am I ugly in the face of society?" I confronted my friend asking him what exactly he meant with that remark. He started laughing: "I was just kidding, man!"

But what if he wasn't kidding? What if his opinion was actually quite close to reality? Even so, is there any benefit in clinging to it and letting it make my life miserable? In some cases, remarks can stalk people for many years. My brother literally has been upset for years about someone he barely knows calling him superficial. I know my brother quite well and I know that he is anything but superficial. At the same time, he has great social skills and the ability to keep things light and fun in conversation. Probably that person saw him as superficial based on his external appearance, which is just one of the many masks we all wear in different situations. The reason my brother was so upset is that he was too attached to the story he tells himself about himself, and also because of sudden fearful thoughts about the future: "What if I am superficial?" and "What will happen to me if I am really superficial?" He carried that insult with him for years. He clung to it. And, therefore, he handed over the power over his faculty to the insulter.

Letting a baseless insult own you after many years is definitely a form of unhealthy attachment. How I handled the high school bullying the years afterward isn't any better. Even though it was just a one-and-a-half-year period, I'd been hurting myself many years after that, by thinking about it and beating myself up. What a waste of time and energy!

I believe that if we would all develop a healthy

detachment towards the world, our lives would be so much better. No one would be murdered anymore because they have insulted someone's mother, targets of bullying wouldn't still suffer from what happened many years ago, religious people wouldn't be bothered if someone portrays their sacred figures in a cartoon, and there would definitely be fewer bar fights. Less trauma, less suicide, less violence, less war.

Funnily enough, as I'm writing this, I'm sitting in the town library and I notice this guy that said some pretty nasty things to me in high school sitting only a few meters away. I felt resentment towards him for many years after I graduated from high school. I even swore revenge one day. Strangely, now that I see him in front of me large as life, I don't feel any resentment. I just see a guy working on his laptop, probably with daily struggles similar to mine, trying to make a living. He was a huge asshole back in the day. Perhaps he still is. I've definitely been an asshole myself as well throughout the years. I've bullied people, I've vented my anger on loved ones, I've talked badly behind other people's backs, I've made people cry. And I know that my own a-holeness was a product of my suffering, my ignorance, my inability to see how I'm hurting others. If I can forgive myself, shouldn't I forgive him too? Well, at least I'm not going to give this guy the power and pleasure to affect me.

Chapter 6 – Insult-proof Confidence

In the previous chapter, we explored the importance of maintaining our own faculty and the power of indifference. We discussed why these things are important to enter the mighty inner circle of unoffendables. Now it's time to take a look at one of the most overhyped self-improvement phenomena: confidence. What is confidence? Can it aid us in handling insults? Or can being confident actually backfire?

False confidence

After I finished high school I wanted to drastically change my personality. I wanted to be more socially involved, so I could develop friendships and success with women. My inner-scholar went on a quest for information on how to improve. On the internet, I stumbled upon different websites like Speed Seduction and sosuave.net, which still exist and offer men advice on how to develop 'game,' seduce women, become desirable and, basically, improve their social life.

Within these communities, men encouraged each other to engage in 'fieldwork' to gain more experience interacting with women. This led to me hanging around shopping centers and bars (oftentimes accompanied by my friend Hamid), and actively approaching a large number of women. This was both scary and fulfilling at the same time. Chatting up a girl you don't know and getting her phone number is absolutely rewarding for the ego, although I rarely phoned these girls. I either preferred the chase over the actual dating itself or I was simply too scared to take the next step. Nevertheless, these experiences were life-changing because I knew that I could approach women and I learned how to handle rejection. Rejection is the biggest reason that people don't approach someone they find attractive. The idea that this person doesn't like you and isn't attracted to you can really crush your ego. But why should they? Attraction is based on personal preferences. If someone isn't attracted to you, how could you possibly take offense?

During my expedition in the seduction world, I learned that there's one thing you must have to be successful with women: confidence. I also discovered that confidence is one of the most multi-explainable concepts ever. The Cambridge dictionary's definition of confidence is this: "the quality of being certain of your abilities or of having trust in people, plans, or the future." Wow. Before I go deeper into this definition I'd like to tell you how I developed false confidence based on a complete misunderstanding of this concept and taking bad advice from the megabytes of material we find on the worldwide web.

Confidence is often explained as a set of behavioral characteristics rather than a state of mind. From this point of view, being confident means talking in a certain way, walking in a certain way, looking a certain way, taking a certain bodily posture, being a leader or a so-called 'alpha male.' I won't deny that walking straight, being well-dressed and well-groomed, being cocky and funny and being the life of the party will increase a man's chances with women. Each of these characteristics can be enhanced and trained. We can get a nice haircut and buy decent clothes, we can go to the gym to improve our bodies and posture and we can practice our social skills. All of this is great, but it doesn't necessarily equate with confidence. It's true that when we've become more socially experienced that we might become more confident about our social skills. But it's also true that someone can have all the social skills and still be very insecure. The reverse happens as well. Someone with lousy social skills can be very secure about them. We can call these people 'overconfident,' where they have an inflated sense of what they really can do.

Personas and masks

In my quest to becoming more confident, I adopted a set of characteristics. I created an image and desperately tried to be that image. I've even looked for people that embodied that image in the movies, television shows, and real-life, and started studying them to the point that I could emulate them down to the last detail. I copied the way they spoke, their facial expressions, their body movements, their style of dressing. I believed that, when I simply imitated confident people, I would be perceived as confident. This is partially true. The 'fake-it-till-you-make-it-approach' works to some extent. The side-effect, however, was that putting on an act all the time that was so at variance with my 'former self' was very exhausting. What I had created was a *persona*, a stage version of me. But this image began to show cracks whenever I built closer relationships with people and couldn't hide behind the mask anymore.

The problem with creating a persona is that we have to continually maintain our narrative about ourselves and how the world sees us. We are encouraged to make 'positive affirmations.' Before I would leave the house I would tell myself things like 'I'm confident,' 'I'm successful' and 'I'm a cocky jerk.' I wore these shiny black shoes, a long black jacket and a thin white scarf that exuded this confidence and success. I walked around like I was the successor of some North-Korean supreme leader. In reality, I had minus €2000 in my bank account, hardly any work experience, no serious relationship experience, accumulating debt rather than wealth and the distinction of being kicked out of college twice because I didn't perform. My confidence was baseless, except for the story I told myself. And when this self-image was threatened, I feared that the real 'me' would be exposed. Behind the façade hid an extremely insecure, fragile young man of low self-worth. This real 'me' was also a story, but much stronger, denser and grown out of years of conditioning. Ashamed of that story, I created a new self-image. But the trouble was the new image was just as fragile and unsustainable. "He who stands on his tiptoes does not stand firm," Lao Tzu once wrote, which surely applied to me.

Creating a self-image has added value in that it helps us cover the dark truth about ourselves. But is that confidence or a lack thereof? A short-term solution to a long standing problem? These short-term solutions never work and will only bite us in the rear in the long run. To live that lie, we must keep people at a distance because, if they came any closer, they would discover some deep dark secret. The more we feed the story we tell ourselves, the more the ego inflates. The root emotion of the ego is fear. People with large egos are easily offended because the ego feels threatened by insults. Oftentimes, an insult is a direct attack on the image we have so carefully crafted to live with ourselves.

The way we handle compliments is another

factor that shapes the ego. Not too long ago I had some female coworkers that complimented me on my looks multiple times. Initially, this was an ego boost – I suddenly felt way more handsome and immediately incorporated the trait of "being handsome" into my self-image. The problem with this is that, when someone doesn't think I'm handsome, my self-image is threatened. The same is true for my YouTube channel. People sometimes overwhelm me with compliments. While I start to think that I'm really as great as these people say, negative comments come in to threaten this self-image. I will take someone bad-mouthing my work as a hit directed at my core.

Big egos at work are a regular phenomenon at the gym. The majority of people in the gym where I train are either scrawny or moderately built. Often I see a buff guy entering the weight room, aware that he's the most muscular guy around. It's very clear to me that his ego uses this observation to dominate the other egos in the room. Indeed, other egos look at him in admiration or envy. When the buff guy notices that he's being watched, his ego and dominance surge to the ceiling. He struts around, performing one feat after another, knowing that he truly is 'the shit.' But then, suddenly, a buffer guy enters. Now, the dominance shifts to the new champion, which simultaneously demotes the lesser fellow. His ego takes a hit and you see him literally shrink.

A Stoic approach to confidence

As you might know by now, the Stoics teach us that external things are beyond our control. Reputation, people's opinions, our physiques are not up to us. What role does this observation play when it comes to confidence? Let's take another look at the Cambridge dictionary's definition of confidence: "the quality of being certain of your abilities or of having trust in people, plans, or the future."

According to the Stoics, we may not control the outside world but we do control our own actions. When we want to learn to play the piano, for example, we control how much time we practice but we can't augment our inherent talent. We can, however, observe if we can please the audience after doing several performances. At the same time, we do not control the audience's reaction – a standing ovation in one place and polite clapping in another. What we do know is that we can play the piece. This is true confidence. We are certain about our ability despite the outcome, as opposed to false confidence which is mere projection.

I'm fairly certain about my ability to edit a video. Also, I'm certain about my Dutch language skills. Why? Because I've been practicing these skills for ages and I've become so experienced that I'm confident about them. I'm also quite confident in regards to playing soccer, creating applications and running long distances: I'm quite confident that I suck at these things. I'm also confident that I may (slightly) improve these skills if I work at them. Knowing that you can do something and cannot do something is confidence. No matter how we apply it, 'Stoic confidence' relates to our own actions and does not relate to the stuff that's not up to us.

Why trust?

There's yet another dimension to confidence, namely, having trust in people, plans, or the future. Like confidence, trust is a multi-faceted term. For some people 'trusting someone' means that the person they trust does exactly what such people want. If this person fails to do this, the trust is broken. Stoics would say that, because we do not control the outside world, this kind of trust can always be broken. In many cases, people are untrustworthy, cheating in relationships, for example. Even the decision to completely trust a significant other is not a guarantee that they will not cheat. Therefore does trust make any sense? Why should I trust someone if that doesn't guarantee it won't happen? Furthermore, controlling people's behavior turns them off because it makes them feel untrustworthy and unfree. Ironically, this only enhances the chances of infidelity.

So, if the future is uncertain and if we cannot control the object of our trust, why should we trust at all? Well, because (and this may sound weird) trust is the only logical position we can take towards a world that is out of whack. Trust is the act of giving up control over the things that are not up to us anyway. Instead of wasting our energy trying to control the object of our affection, we simply let it slide. This doesn't mean that we shouldn't take action to get what we want. Prophet Muhammad once said: "Have faith in God, but tie your camel."

A friend of mine, whom we'll call Jack, once explained to me his attitude towards relationships, which opened my eyes. He told me that he deliberately chooses to trust his girlfriend, simply because it isn't up to him what she does and whether she speaks the truth or not. Thus, as long as there's no clear evidence that she is cheating or lying, he hardly thinks about these possibilities. Jack had no problem with her traveling alone for a few months in Southeast Asia and sharing her hotel rooms with other travelers to mitigate the cost. Except for the fact that he's worried about her safety sometimes, he doesn't worry about the possibility of her cheating at all. I asked him if that wasn't a bit naïve – I for one would have been very suspicious. "The things is," said Jack solemnly, "you simply don't know what happens. Maybe she did cheat. Maybe not. Unless she admits that she did, you simply do not know. So, why worry about it?" Well, that was a clear example of 'Stoic trust' that bowled me over at the time.

Now, what has all this to do with confidence? First of all, the ability to let things go and not worry about them is a form of confidence already. It means that you are confident that you simply do not know a lot of things, that you are confident that the outside world is out of control, and that you can choose whether to torment yourself by worry or not. Another aspect is the confidence that you can handle the outcome, whatever this may be. This is basically what we call 'trust in yourself.' If we can be 'okay' with the outcome – no matter what it is – what's there left to worry about? This is amor fati.

The power of vulnerability

Confidence is a sense of certainty about the things we can do but also about the things we cannot do. This leaves us room to be vulnerable. 'Vulnerability' can be a vessel for personal growth. We know that we aren't perfect and probably lacking in numerous things and we are realistic about that. Only by accepting our limitations can we move further.

Anna, for example, suffers from social anxiety.

She also stammers when talking to strangers, and wants to improve her condition. However, because she is so ashamed of her stammering, she avoids social interaction altogether, so she doesn't have to deal with the problem. This leads to the vicious circle of her social anxiety increasing her stammer, while her stammer increases her social anxiety. The one reinforces the other. By being vulnerable, she will be opening herself to the big bad out-of-control world full of opinions, jerks, judgment and abuse. Can she afford to take the risk? Will it make matters worse?

Ironically, making herself vulnerable could be the only way to go for things to get better. When she rises up and confronts the very thing she fears – social disapproval – the anxiety eventually goes away. And as the anxiety goes, the stammering subsides. So, what should she do? If she is confident about her situation, she should fully embrace her true self with all her imperfections. She will not be deterred by some jerks making fun of her and laughing about her behind her back; these things aren't up to her anyway and what other people think is none of her business. This allows her to breathe. Now that the great burden of shame is lifted from her shoulders, she can focus on what she can control: her own actions. Her vulnerability has set her free.

A few years ago I was at a Toastmasters meeting and I sat beside a guy who stammers. Despite his stammering, he gives speech after speech, travels the world, obtained a master's degree in marketing and currently has a well-paying job as an online marketer. Sure, he is aware of his stammering. But he's also aware of his intelligence and his skills. If he hadn't made himself vulnerable by not pursuing his goal out of fear of judgment, he would never have become so successful. We can run away from our dark side but then we'll run away from our bright side as well. When we deny ourselves, we will not live up to our potential.

The ancient Stoics did not write about confidence specifically but they did write about courage and cowardice. Courage is a virtue and cowardice is a vice. In many ways, confidence is an act of courage. Living in accordance with the metaphysical truth of what's up to us and what's not up to us takes courage. It means that we take full responsibility for our own actions and cannot blame others for our blunders. Fully accepting ourselves and being vulnerable takes courage because, in doing so, we are stepping out from the shadow and are exposing ourselves to the light. We will not just expose ourselves to the world but to ourselves as well. But we can comfort ourselves with the thought that the only certainty we have about life is that it is uncertain. How courageous it is to face uncertainty and be receptive to whatever comes at us!

To tie it all in: Stoic confidence is not a set of behaviors, nor is it an inflated sense of self-esteem. It's about maintaining equilibrium regardless of outcome. If we are confident about ourselves, our position in the universe and the fact that we'll thrive no matter what, how can we possibly be thrown off balance by the brickbats of the uninitiated?

Chapter 7 – The Art of Letting Go

"The unhappy man is always absent from himself, never present to himself. But one can be absent, obviously, either in the past or in the future. This adequately circumscribes the entire territory of the unhappy consciousness."

~ Søren Kierkegaard, *Either & Or*
(first published in 1843 and the translation
by Alastair Hannay was published in 1992)

When we observe the active mind closely it becomes clear that it often acts like a hyperactive orangutan jumping from branch to branch. The majority of people suffer from an illness called excessive thinking, which can be described as repetitive thinking patterns that are for the greater part obsolete and, above all, destructive. The way we feel depends on the quality of our thoughts. When we are perpetually plagued by negative memories, we feel miserable. When we worry about the future, we feel anxious. In both cases people often seek relief in alcohol, drugs, binge-watching series on Netflix, playing video games, watching porn and other activities that occupy the mind so it is temporarily relieved of its own destructive tendencies. The mind loves problems. When there is a lack of problems it can chew on, the mind will create new ones, regardless of how this affects us emotionally.

We can experience a moment of inner peace until the mind says: "Hey you! Do you remember what your ex-boyfriend did after he already cheated on you twice? Exactly. He lied about that female coworker, too. What a jerk, isn't he?" By initiating this thought, the mind is basically sending you an invitation to chat. Or rather, a spam message. The mind is literally phishing for attention. When I worked at the online banking security department of a large Dutch bank, I used to speak with angry clients who sometimes blamed us for spam that was sent on behalf of our bank. When that happened I had to explain that the bank doesn't control emails or WhatsApp messages that outside parties send to them, including phishing. Anyone can send a phishing message, right? The only thing a bank can do is teach its clients that phishing emails are attempts to obtain personal information to access their bank account, and the best way to handle these attempts is by not responding.

The same is true with our thoughts. We cannot control the mind sending us these chat requests. But we can control our response. This means that there is a distinction between the mind and that which observes the mind. The former sends the chat invitations, the latter accepts them. The former is beyond our control; the latter is within our control. Thus, we can conclude that the latter is us, and we are a separate entity from our thoughts. If there wasn't a distinction, how could it be that we can have conversations with ourselves?

The mind is a powerful tool. We can use it to solve puzzles, to survive in the world, for science. But the mind can also be our greatest enemy. An untrained mind keeps accepting those chat requests because it cannot separate thinking from random observations. We are not our thoughts. Rather, we are supposed to use thoughts to solve problems when necessary. Unfortunately, in many cases our thoughts use us. An untrained mind is highly susceptible to insults. Insults intrigue the problem-seeking mind. An insult for the mind is like caviar to a king, a delicacy. I mean, is there anything that can arouse the thinking mind more than a nasty, backhanded compliment from an annoying coworker? This can propel the mind to create dozens of thoughts, most of them not very positive. Some insults can feed the mind for years, recycling the same scenes over and over again, generating the same emotions. "*Any person capable of angering you becomes your master; he can anger you only when you permit yourself to be disturbed by him*," said Epictetus.

When my brother was called superficial, he permitted this person to disturb him to the extent that years later his mind was still under the spell of this remark. When his thoughts sent him the invitation to chat about this remark, he accepted it without hesitation, leading to yet another round of frustration, self-doubt, self-hate, anger, resentment and whatever other emotions the endless chatter about his superficiality generated. If his mind had been trained, he could have discarded its requests to chat about things that make him miserable. The same is true of the coworker who called me "snatsy," which kept my mind overthinking and overanalyzing for hours on end.

Marcus Aurelius once wrote: "*if you are distressed by anything external, the pain is not due to the thing itself, but to your estimate of it; and this you have the power to revoke at any moment.*" An untrained mind does not realize that it has the power to estimate the value of the insults. When we realize that many nasty remarks come from a place of ignorance, fear or anger, we know that they don't carry a lot of value, and we might as well discard them. Thus, before we get offended, we might want to ask ourselves what benefits come from that. Let's say someone insults us. Whether or not the insult is true, what's the point of thinking about it repeatedly? Does this solve anything? Probably not.

The mind and the shadow

Swiss psychiatrist Carl Jung noticed that, because a tremendous amount of thinking happens in the unconscious, many thoughts rarely see the light of day. These thoughts are often inconvenient or worse: downright evil. According to Jung, everyone carries a shadow, though many don't realize that they do. Most of us seem to identify with the masks we wear, which we have also called our *persona*. This is a set of characteristics and beliefs that we want to present to the outside world. At the same time, we repress thoughts and behaviors we don't want the world to see. The danger is that the shadow may come to the surface uncontrollably and cause a lot of damage. Thus, Jung stated that we must integrate the shadow in our personality to work with it, and thereby gain control

Jung's observation is essential to becoming unoffendable in that, by acknowledging that the shadow is part of the human experience, we might become more compassionate towards those that are controlled by the shadow: the jerks, the bullies, the abusers, and so forth. The second reason is that, by seeing the shadow in ourselves, we will know that we, too, have a dark side which causes us to be quickly offended.

A striking attribute of having a dense shadow is the tendency to project our own unwanted characteristics onto other people. My mother's alcoholic ex-boyfriend used to hate weakness in males. He used to call us youngsters and his own two sons "wimps" constantly, especially when we cried about something. But later I figured out that he was terribly weak himself and that he had been physically abused by his father, who couldn't stand his weaknesses either. Hence, he needed liquid courage to mask his own shortcomings, while his shadow projected them onto people. Eventually, he drank himself to death.

Perhaps the greatest example of projection I've seen is from the movie *American Beauty*. [SPOILER ALERT] Retired U.S. Marine colonel Frank Fitts is malignantly homophobic, saying things like: "How come these faggots always have to rub it in your face? How come they're so shameless?" At the end of the movie, it becomes clear that Frank himself has been repressing his own homosexuality all his life. This is the result of a culture in which men and women are expected to conform to strong gender roles; everything that goes against these roles ends up in the shadow. The more we repress, the more things start to well up beneath the surface. It's no surprise that this attitude led to Fitts murdering the protagonist Lester Burnham, who discovered Fitt's homosexuality quite by accident [END SPOILER].

Awareness

The good thing is that, once we become aware of the shadow, we can discover why we become offended. We'll be more aware of why we behave in certain ways. I'm a firm believer that only by awareness can we work with the shadow, and even turn our negatives into positives. Psychologist Marion Woodman observed that the shadow doesn't solely contain negative things but it is also a source of positive things that have been repressed over the years. Like creativity, "the night is as precious as is the day," Woodman said. The shadow may harbor huge amounts of energy that can be harvested for a good cause.

My friend Barry, for example, told me recently about certain experiences in his youth which made him explode easily when someone mocked him. He somehow found a way to channel this explosive energy into sports and his career. Similarly, my friend Hamid once admitted that his experiences with racism made him decide never to be treated badly again. Taking a deep look at his life thus far, he decided to put his energy into his ambitions, and later found relief in religion. The former led to a fantastic career in marketing. The latter transformed him from an angry, short-tempered guy to someone with compassion and patience.

Another great example of successful shadow integration is my youngest brother who had a difficult youth, especially when we lived with our alcoholic stepfather. In 2010 he served in the war in Afghanistan. When he was on patrol his vehicle got hit by an IED. Not only was he the driver of the vehicle, he was the only survivor, losing one of his best buddies. Long after he recovered physically, he was still filled with rage and guilt. With the help of therapy and his own iron willpower, he turned his shadow into one accomplishment after another; whether in sports, work or personal relationships.

I've been working with my own shadow to this day. Among other things, past bullying, traumatic experiences in my youth, my love-hate relationship with my father and bad experiences with women have led to an extremely dense shadow to the point that I've had desires to either kill myself or hurt another person out of revenge. It also turned me temporarily into an angry misogynistic jerk that just wanted to see the world burn. On top of that, I've been a problem drinker for years with quite a track record of nasty, idiotic, disrespectful acts, followed by terrible hangovers and one alcohol poisoning event that nearly cost me my life. Needless to say, I'm very happy that I'm doing much better now. While I'm writing this, I haven't touched a drink for months. In the meantime, I've been writing, meditating, exercising and directing the wisdom that I've found valuable into videos that I publish on my YouTube channel.

Now, how do we shed light on what's lurking in the darkness? I can attest to the fact that meditation is a powerful method to train the mind. Basic meditation practice is the act of sitting still for a certain period, observing the breath as well as what's happening in the mind without judgment. Even though meditation is originally a Buddhist practice, it's been secularized and frequently applied by non-Buddhist practitioners. By practicing meditation one learns to know the mind, train the mind and eventually free the mind. This means that we examine not only our superficial thought processes but also the ones in the back of our minds secretly lurking in the darkness. The essence of meditation is 'mindfulness.' Mindfulness is the mental state of being conscious and aware of the present moment.

Aside from meditation, we can use the quality of being mindful in our daily lives and in activities like working, driving and talking to people. By doing this, we not only become aware of our surroundings but also of the inner world. Take, for instance, when our shadow is triggered because we get offended by, let's say, a nasty insult, how does the body react to the insult? Do we observe any emotions? If so, what do we feel? Do we feel angry? Intimidated?

I remember countless occasions in which a simple remark spun a complete drama in my head that could go on for weeks. A pertinent example is an incident that happened at the start of my last year in college where I was studying for a bachelor's degree. I was placed in a small project group of four people, three guys and a girl. One of these guys was very extroverted and had been diagnosed with ADHD. He basically said whatever came to his mind before thinking about it. I'm probably the opposite, being introverted and always weighing things before I speak, so it always requires some degree of calibration to get along with such people. I think that relationships between introverted and extroverted people are the most interesting ones because they complement each other in many ways. The ADHD guy wasn't slow in giving his opinion, telling me laughingly that he thought I look Moroccan. He repeated this a few times in the weeks that followed. I was extremely offended, even though one of my best friends Hamid is actually Moroccan.

One day I got angry at the ADHD guy. He was startled by my outburst. His remarks weren't meant as an insult; it was just something that occurred to him and seemed funny. He couldn't really understand why I was so offended. The truth is that I began heating up slowly from the first time he made that remark, and after about four times I reached boiling point. My shadow took over.

A similar example was an incident during work in that warehouse I told you about. One day, a tall, big guy started work there and became my direct colleague. He was a convicted felon freshly out of prison, who had been given another chance in the workforce. And they weren't petty crimes. Nonetheless, I liked the guy and he liked me so we became buddies. A strange combination but it worked. One day I got very angry at him because he had started calling me 'Ali.' Ali is a Middle Eastern name that he used to mock my Middle Eastern looks. After a few times, I just blew up in front of him. Imagine a 6 foot 5 hardened (former) criminal completely startled by a short, nerdy guy exploding in rage. He was seriously hurt seeing from the redness in his eyes. "I understand. But you didn't have to say it that way," he said. Like the ADHD guy, he couldn't understand what set me off. From his perception calling me 'Ali' was just nothing more than a good humored tease. In my mind, however, he turned from friend to enemy from the moment he started calling me that. Why was I so upset? How come that any comment on my exotic looks seemed to be my kryptonite?

After these incidents, I realized that all references to my Middle Eastern looks ignite memories of being bullied when I lived in the countryside. I guess that's what my friend Hamid and I had in common. For years I shared with him the same conviction that this anger was righteous. In other words: people should just shut the hell up about my appearance. And if they didn't, I should make them.

Unfortunately, what people say is not up to me. The Stoics repeated over and over that it's not the actions of people that disturb us, but the position we take towards them.

"Think you that the people could do any wrong to such a man when they tore away his praetorship or his toga? When they bespattered his sacred head with the rinsings of their mouths? The wise man is safe, and no injury or insult can touch him."

~ Lucius Annaeus Seneca,
On The Firmness Of The Wise Man, II
(translated by Aubrey Stewart, 1900)

Trying to prevent the world from speaking about my Middle Eastern looks is an impossible goal. The only way to reduce my suffering was to become more resilient. Years later I began to see what processes caused this suffering by observing my thoughts. I became aware of the fact that when someone made a joke about my appearance, I would feel threatened instantly. Painful memories would arise in my mind: the high school bullying, the racism I've experienced in the rural areas, the humiliation, feeling excluded and less of a person. I started having thoughts like: "Here we go again," "It's just a matter of time before people find my weak spot," and "From now on, everyone will be against me." My mind made it clear that it didn't want that. So when it happened I could do two things: fight or flight. I didn't want to be a coward, so I preferred to fight. In my head, that is. I began thinking about how I should tell that person to shut up, how to bully that person back, how to humiliate that person, how to hurt that person. I just wanted to take that person down. In my thoughts, there was a lot at stake. But most of this – if not all – was me clinging to an illusion created by the mind.

The destructiveness of judging

I remember an evening when I ridiculed an old friend who was crying because his girlfriend broke up with him. At a party, after a few beers, he burst out in tears.

My cousin immediately started comforting and soothing him. I, on the other hand, was standing in the garden calling him a wuss. In reality, I was an emotional wreck myself with immense grief over my own recent breakup which I never showed to the world. The tears came solely in my private space, sometimes, a lot. I think that I judged my friend so harshly because I didn't allow myself to show emotion either. The repression of my own grief caused me to be hard on other men that show weakness.

Jung noted that a dense shadow causes us to be judgmental because we project things onto other people that we don't want to see in ourselves. In the same way, we judge ourselves when we see unwanted thoughts and emotions arise. A woman who projects her repressed homosexuality onto her environment in the form of homophobia probably punishes herself harshly when her own lesbian tendencies come to the surface. If we judge our thoughts and emotions, we basically form an opinion about them. Moreover, we almost judge everything we perceive. For example, you notice that you're sad and think: "I shouldn't be sad." Or, you notice that a past event flashes in your mind and you think: "I shouldn't think about that." By judging some thoughts negatively, we automatically create an aversion towards those thoughts. Thus, every time such a thought arises, we suffer, we punish ourselves and may even begin to hate ourselves. On the other hand, by judging some thoughts positively, we automatically create a desire to have these 'correct' thoughts at the exclusion of everything else.

What's so problematic about judgment is that it prevents the shadow from showing itself. Let's face it: who likes to be judged? I'd say that judging is just another form of repression by letting that part of ourselves know that it's unwanted and unwelcome. This only has the effect of making the shadow denser. The Buddhists practice a neutral non-judgmental observation of their thoughts. Only then can the thoughts can move freely. Only then can the shadow feel safe enough to expose itself. The problem, however, with trying to pull off non-judgmental observations is that we judge the judgments: "I'm judging and that's wrong! I shouldn't judge!"

The morning I wrote this I rode past my old high school by bicycle. Even though I had some great times there, there's still pain looking at that building and schoolyard. It makes me feel those turbulent times at home as well: moving in with an alcoholic, my depressed mother, my angry father. Just looking at the building makes me sad. When this sadness comes upon me, my mind starts to judge: "You shouldn't feel sad. You should be over it. You should leave the past in the past." Then, my mind starts to judge the judging. "Hey, you shouldn't be judgmental about this!" Then, my mind starts to judge the judging of the judging. This mechanism of 'thinking about thinking about thinking' can go on till infinity and only creates anxiety. The trick is not just 'not judging' but 'not judging the judging.' Doing so, makes us observe the mind's judgments without fighting them because we accept that they're just fabrications of the mind like any other form of thought. "Whatever you accept completely, you go beyond. If you fight it, you're stuck with it," says spiritual teacher Eckhart Tolle.

In regards to being offended, we can say it's not the words that offend us but our judgments about those words. Like they did with Frank Fitts, these words might stir up repressed feelings and thoughts. Or past bullying might be the reason that we flare up when someone throws us a playful insult. Examining the workings of our mind and shedding light on what we've hidden in the dark helps us better understand why we are offended by such things.

Caring less what people think

We have been taught our whole lives that outside factors are highly important, sometimes even more important than the inner world. Money often becomes the ultimate concern. For the average Westerner, attaining fame is equivalent to attaining *nirvana* for a Buddhist or *eudaimonia* for a Stoic. People go on shopping sprees thinking that buying a lot of stuff will make them happy. But, like any form of pleasure, the indulgence of the senses is only a temporary fix. The Stoics practice curbing sensual gratification by simplifying their food intake. Instead of the extravagant explosion of flavors that most 'foodies' crave, they don't eat for pleasure but for nourishment. If we eat for pleasure we might begin to rely on food to numb our emotional pain. This is what so-called 'emotional eaters' do. As shopping is for shopaholics, comfort food is their way to deal with their inner pain, including boredom and restlessness. These forms of reliance on external forces may seem extreme, but seeking happiness outside of us instead of inside us is more common than we think.

The whole consumerist thrust of society is aimed at diverting our attention from core issues to the panacea of material things with the notion that this will make us happy. This collective consumerist mindset keeps us on the wheel of exchanging our bodies in the form of labor to buy a lot of stuff we don't need. A fictional character from *Fight Club* named Tyler Durden described this wheel of slavery very well:

"You buy furniture. You tell yourself, this is the last sofa I will ever need in my life. Buy the sofa, then for a couple years you're satisfied that no matter what goes wrong, at least you've got your sofa issue handled. Then the right set of dishes. Then the perfect bed. The drapes. The rug. Then you're trapped in your lovely nest, and the things you used to own, now they own you."

~ Tyler Durden, *Fight Club* (1999)

When we crave for an object, the object of our craving holds us in captivity. It decides our behavior, our emotions, our thoughts. The end justifies the means. We can see an extreme manifestation of this mechanism in addicts. Drug addicts, for example, oftentimes lie, cheat, steal, and even use violence, to get another fix from their drug of choice. The cocaine has enslaved the one seeking to get to the object of his craving. When your happiness relies on the way your food is flavored, you'll be unhappy when you encounter food that's not tasty enough (even though it's nutritious). If your happiness is attached to the position of Bitcoin, the bull market at the end of 2017 probably made you euphoric and the crash that followed in early 2018, miserable.

"The things in our control are by nature free, unrestrained, unhindered; but those not in our control are weak, slavish, restrained, belonging to others," said Epictetus. Stoicism emphasizes that to be happy, we must focus on the things within our control. We don't control outside events like politics and the weather.

Things like property and money can be taken away in a heartbeat. It might be surprising to some, but we don't control our bodies either. Our bodies get sick, age and die. When you're a beautiful woman and your happiness is predominantly linked to your looks, you'll be wretched when your looks begin to fade. I often see that when people become older they find things other than the body that define their happiness, because, in general, an aging body loses its value in the sexual marketplace.

I've already mentioned that the Stoics see a good reputation only as a 'preferred indifferent,' Not as a necessity. To elaborate on the 'preferred indifferent,' the Stoics distinguish between virtue and vice. Virtue can be subdivided into wisdom, justice, courage, and moderation. Vice can be subdivided into foolishness, injustice, cowardice, and intemperance. Virtue leads to happiness. Vice leads to misery. Between virtue and vice, there's a huge gray area. Within this area, we'll find the many things that we do not control, which are either 'preferred indifferents' like wealth, good health and good reputation, or 'dispreferred indifferents' like poverty, illness, and a bad reputation. The Stoics don't deny the impact of all these. However, they don't have to influence our happiness. We can still be very happy even when we have a bad reputation, or very unhappy even when we have a good reputation. How many celebrities aren't in pain despite their fame? It's fine to have preferred indifferents but, according to the Stoics, they shouldn't dictate our life.

"Don't waste the rest of your time here worrying about other people—unless it affects the common good. It will keep you from doing anything useful. You'll be too preoccupied with what so-and-so is doing, and why, and what they're saying, and what they're thinking, and what they're up to, and all the other things that throw you off and keep you from focusing on your own mind."

~ Marcus Aurelius, *Meditations*, Book 3, 4

Weaning from authority figures
After my weird and turbulent twenties, I began to understand that seeking validation from others isn't the way to go. Moreover, connecting my happiness to the actions of other people made me the servant of their whims. I think that my father played a huge role in this,

by demanding a lot from his children and loving us only on certain conditions. For many years I saw it as my purpose to make my father happy and proud. When I succeeded, he showered me with positive attention. But when I screwed up, he withdrew his positive attention and, in some situations, he literally disassociated from me by discarding me as a son. This was a very unhealthy relationship. He viewed his children's obedience as loyalty. In reality, it was slavery.

Our mental programming of seeking validation from an authority figure in everything we do (the people we associate with, the career decisions we make and even the way we view ourselves) is reflected in our general stance towards the world. We become people pleasers. We are highly concerned about the opinions of others. People that take such a stance are very open to manipulation and end up doing things against their will, simply to receive positive strokes from others. It took me time and effort to disconnect my personal sense of contentment from my father's demands. After that, I depended less and less on what my friends, family members, coworkers, and other people thought about me. While a friend's dislike could have been disastrous in the past, it's just a 'dispreferred indifferent' today. I still do care, though. I believe it's hard, if not impossible, to be completely unmoved by what others think and say about us. The key is to stop clinging to the thoughts and emotions that arise when someone insults us, speaks ill about us, betrays us, ridicules us, or in whatever way 'wrongs' us. Today I just think: "What other people think is none of my business."

Anger issues

We now know that when we are offended it's not the offender's fault but ours for choosing to hold on to the negative thoughts and emotions that arise from being offended. It takes a clear mind to observe one's thoughts and emotional reactions, make the distinction between the observer and the thoughts, know that we aren't our thoughts, and choose to let the mind's fabrications go.

I've observed that intoxicants, like alcohol, impede the mind's ability not only to discern right from

163

wrong but also to separate us from our thoughts and emotions. When we're drunk, we function in a very unconscious and primal way. This causes us to act upon negative thoughts and emotions a lot quicker without questioning the validity of them or the consequences of our actions. Like dogs, we feel a certain desire 'now' so we must act on this desire 'now.' In many cases, infidelity happens under the influence of alcohol. So do physical as well as verbal disputes. Needless to say, I've had the worst fights when I was drunk. My feelings of rage were so intense that I didn't see any other option other than letting them out of my system.

Years later, I asked myself: is that so strange when you've lost your consciousness? Even without being in a state of intoxication, I've had great difficulty in containing angry outbursts. My ex-girlfriends have suffered a lot because I wasn't able to see beyond the rising emotions when something provoked me. I felt that my anger was righteous. But it wasn't. There's no righteous anger. I'd like to share a Buddhist simile that explains why.

Once upon a time, there was a young boy with anger issues. His father gave him a bag of nails along with the following instructions: "Every time you get angry, you must hit a nail in the fence." So, he did. The first few days he hit dozens of nails into the fence. But as the days passed, this number began to lessen. One day he didn't become angry at all. He proudly told his father that day that he didn't lose his temper even once. His father then told him to pull out one nail from the fence each day he was able to hold his temper.

Weeks later the boy happily told his father that all the nails were gone. As father and son stood at the fence, the father said: "Well done, my son. Now I want you to look at the fence closely. Do you see all the holes? The fence will never be the same. Anger always leaves a mark. You can stick a knife into someone's body and pull it out. But no matter how much you apologize, the scar will be there until death."

This too shall pass

It took the passage of time when I reached the age of thirty before I realized that my anger has done irreparable damage. Even when people forgive you, your deeds will alter their relationship towards you. We won't be angry at the fire when it burns us, but we will avoid it in the future. I've burnt many bridges because of my anger. Luckily, I discovered that there's a way to manage my emotions. An essential realization to settle this is to think about the nature of impermanence.

If you've ever encountered someone with Borderline Personality Disorder (BPD) you've seen what the inability to regulate emotions can do to that person's behavior. People that cannot regulate their emotions are triggered by almost everything they encounter – no matter how trivial. It's no secret that people with BPD experience emotions much more intensely, which makes it a lot harder to regulate them. If a simple insult feels like being cut into two by a knife, how much more difficult must it be to not engage with the pain and anger that it causes? This is the reason why such intense pain is often regulated by physical pain that literally cuts with a knife. Can you imagine how much emotional hurt these people must have been through to resort to such methods?

In the latest psychiatric methods, the practice of mindfulness has become an essential therapy for people that suffer from BPD. By applying mindfulness they learn to observe their thoughts and emotions instead of instantly venting them. They learn to see that thoughts are just fabrications of the mind that come and go, and emotions are sensations in the body as a consequence of thought. But, to trust in the effectiveness of this method, we must basically 'know' that everything is in flux. We must trust that the nature of our inner world is set up in a way that thoughts, as well as emotions, come and go. The way our bodily sensations move is in accordance with the ever-changing universe which is entropic in nature. Thus, nothing is permanent, nothing remains.

To see the truth in this, we only have to observe our surroundings very closely. Watch the seasons come and go, civilizations rise and fall, people being born and dying. The appearance and disappearance of the human body happen in the same fashion as other fruits of nature, like animals and apples. We start out small, grow and, after we've achieved full growth, begin to decay. Philosopher Alan Watts said that just as an apple tree produces apples, the earth produces people. Thus, like an apple tree is 'appling' the earth is 'peopling.'

Impermanence can frighten us but it can also relieve us. It's just a matter of how we choose to see it. When we have a conservation mentality towards everything that 'is' we won't welcome change all that readily simply because we desire for things to stay as they are. However, when we welcome and see the joy of change, we'll not be bothered by impermanence. We may be saddened to know that the great moments don't last. But, at the same time, we may be very happy that moments of misery don't either.

There's a Sufi story about a king whose happiness depended on the prosperity of the kingdom. When times were bad, he was depressed and often retreated to his private quarters for escape from the outside world. When times were good he was very joyful and outgoing, and threw extravagant parties in the palace. One fine day, because he couldn't tolerate his mood swings any longer, he summoned the wisest men of the kingdom. He asked them to create a ring for him that would make him happy when he was sad. So, they did. Days later the wise men handed over a ring with the following sentence etched on it: "This too shall pass." It worked. In times of despair, the king simply looked at his ring, just to learn that the impermanence of the universe would eventually end the kingdom's misery. Conversely, when times were good, the ring reminded him that impermanence would end the kingdom's prosperity as well. This made him more circumspect about losing himself in his joy when times were great, and prepare himself for darker times instead.

Our thoughts and emotions are impermanent. No matter how immersed you are in your anger right now, or how much you hate a specific person, it's all temporary. Unfortunately, the more we are caught up in our emotions, the less likely it seems that, at some point, this mindstate (whether negative or positive) will pass. This is especially true of the euphoria involved with the phenomenon of 'romantic love.' Falling in love for the first time, people often think that this out-of-the-world feeling for one another will last forever. And when it doesn't last, they simply fall in love with the next person, thinking, "This time, it will last."

But this euphoria, also known as the 'honeymoon phase' never lasts. It simply evolves into something different, which is either sustainable or not.

This doesn't mean that we shouldn't enjoy the experience; but the problems arise when we cling to it. Some people are literally addicted to romantic love. They jump from person to person to perpetually stay on that high, just as an alcoholic cleaves to his beer. But when the object of our fix isn't available anymore, the period of infatuation will inevitably be followed by a low. People who've fallen in love multiple times (like myself) probably know by now that the honeymoon phase doesn't last. That's why we know that it's much healthier to enjoy romance with minimal attachment to that pleasurable feeling, which, in turn, can be done by soberly remembering the nature of impermanence.

We can approach our bodily sensations in a similar way. It's not the sensations themselves that cause problems but our clinging to them. When we are angry because someone offends us, we might think that 'doing something' is the only path to relief. We might kick someone's ass, we might scream and yell, we might punch the wall, thinking that this somehow helps to 'let the anger out.' Well, it doesn't. If anything, it will only make it worse. We might be fooled into thinking that acting out helps diffuse the anger because ten minutes later it has disappeared.

But the reality is that impermanence has done a great job in making the anger subside naturally after we've drained our energy by acting out. Acting out and anger subsiding aren't the same thing. If we pay attention closely, we'll notice that the one happens after the other and never at the same time. The problem is that, by acting out we're leaving scars, like the holes in the fence created by the nails in the Buddhist story. Isn't it better to skip that stage, and go straight for the subsiding of our emotions? If that's what we want, the only way is to let our emotions be, without judging, clinging to or interfering with them. And the universe will do the rest.

Chapter 8 – Facing the Trolls

So we're starting to transform the mind by changing the way we think. In the previous chapters, I focused on empathy, compassion, and acceptance. Many times, people don't mean to insult us. Also, the inability to accept different opinions leads to people feeling offended, which may lead to censorship. But this doesn't mean that people can't be immense jerks that are out to insult, offend, and ridicule you. This species is known as trolls. It's time to put ourselves out there and practice facing these trolls.

Most trolls are only harmful to the degree that you make them. Some just like to make fun of people; others are really out there to indulge in sadistic power play. When I was a kid I always believed that adults in general (except for true villains like Adolf Hitler) would be mature enough to not purposefully make the lives of others miserable. I thought that the majority of grown-ups would be all compassionate, pleasant, friendly people and that they would hardly engage in bullying each other. Boy, was I wrong! Jerks are everywhere in any age group. Whether we're at work, in a store, in prison, at university or at the sports club, there's always a bunch of ill-willed, nasty, rude, selfish specimens out there. Even retirement homes are not spared from trolls. I know of a retirement home in Rotterdam that made a lot of news in 2017 because of a group of residents intimidating the rest by cursing and discrimination. Bullying turns out to be very common among the elderly, mainly because they're frustrated about being put away in the first place.

Less offended, more respectful

In the previous chapters, I talked about the inner work of becoming unoffendable. I discussed the fact that, if we've done our inner work right, we'd most likely be less validation-seeking, less attached to what people say and more focused on the things within our control. Nonetheless, I admit that it takes some practice to be truly less affected when encountering trolls in real life. Luckily, there are many things we can do to build a mindset that's resilient and skillful when dealing with difficult people.

This chapter focuses on methods of dealing with trolls in the most efficient, passive and peaceful ways. The key to being resilient against jerks and a-holes is the understanding that that no matter where we go, we most likely will encounter undesirable people. After accepting this, we can move on to a series of techniques that help us to deal with them.

Using negativity as preparation

It may sound a bit strange to incorporate negativity to reach a positive outcome. But if we realize that the world is made out of negatives and positives, then it's logical to include both of them. The ancient Taoist work, the *Tao Te Ching,* shows us that positive and negative always complement one another. The Taoists call these forces *yin* and *yang*, which are also seen as the feminine and the masculine. Yin and yang always seek balance. Thus, when there's a positive spike, then there's always a negative spike as well. Being high on XTC, for example, leads to a spike in happy feelings. But when this high wears off, the body balances itself by going into a state of depression. The term 'blue

Monday' points to the hangover that follows after using XTC over the weekend. The more you use, the bluer the Monday will be.

Another example is how we create value judgments about our world, like what's ugly and what's beautiful. While beauty is collectively desired above ugliness, there cannot be beauty without ugliness. When we remove everything that is ugly, it follows that what's beautiful has nothing to compare against to justify being called beautiful. The spindle that previously separated beauty and ugliness will move to a new center, and the part that was regarded as beauty will now inhabit the domain of the ugly. Lao Tzu, the author of the *Tao Te Ching* states:

"Being and non-being produce each other.
Difficult and easy complement each other.
Long and short define each other.
High and low oppose each other.
Fore and aft follow each other."

~ Lao Tzu, *Tao Te Ching*, chapter 2
(translated by John H. McDonald)

We can apply these modulations to human expectations as well. When we have high expectations, anything of lesser value happening in the future will be a disappointment. When we have low expectations, everything of lesser value happening in the future will be a disappointment as well but, because our expectations are low, there are more things that will not be a disappointment. Optimism can, therefore, be quite dangerous. When we walk out of the door expecting the world to be great, then reality will undoubtedly slap us in the face. But when we walk out of the door expecting the world to not be so great, it'll probably be better than expected. Now, intense and deep negative feelings probably won't even get us past the front door, so I wouldn't recommend that. Being overly optimistic is also a recipe for disappointment. On the other hand, if we can internalize the right amount of negativity, we create a method of coping with a world full of jerks. Because we instill negativity within ourselves, we actually become receptive to positivity. Instead of filling ourselves to the brim with desires about how fantastic the people around us will be, we don't expect too much and, thus, every joyful encounter we have will be a blessing.

Marcus Aurelius built a powerful morning exercise called the *praemeditatio malorum* (translated 'negative visualization') which goes like this:

"When you wake up in the morning, tell yourself: The people I deal with today will be meddling, ungrateful, arrogant, dishonest, jealous, and surly. They are like this because they can't tell good from evil."

~ Marcus Aurelius, *Meditations*, Book 2, 1

Stoic philosopher Epictetus proposed a similar thought exercise that is presented less often as a model for negative visualization:

"When you are going about any action, remind yourself what nature the action is. If you are going to bathe, picture to yourself the things which usually happen in the bath: some people splash the water, some push, some use abusive language, and others steal. Thus you will more safely go about this action if you say to yourself, 'I will now go bathe, and keep my own mind in a state conformable to nature.' And in the same manner with regard to every other action."

177

~ Epictetus, *Enchiridion*, 4
(translated by Elizabeth Carter, 1758)

The praemeditatio malorum prepares us for the day by accepting that the world isn't all rainbows and butterflies and that we will meet with nasty people one way or the other. When we know that a certain place is full of jerks, we'll be less shocked if we encounter them. Whether or not something bad will happen is always uncertain. But, if it does happen, at least we are prepared. At the same time, the exercise carries a sense of compassion in it by saying, almost in a forgiving way, that a jerk "can't tell good from evil." When we take a closer look at the world around us, we can indeed see that many people are ignorant and that their bad behavior stems from this. Having this knowledge in the forefront of our minds will not only make it easier to be unaffected by bothersome encounters, it will help us to forgive humanity for its flaws as well.

Ignoring and not reacting

Egos like to attack other egos. But when the ego isn't

there, what's there to attack? Most clashes I see are between humans with big egos. Their over-inflated selves don't allow others to be superior to them, criticize them or mock them. In fact, mockery is one of the biggest triggers for the ego because it pushes an overly inflated sense of self-importance into the domain of ridicule. As pointed out earlier in this book, ridicule attacks the story that the person tells itself. Being mocked, therefore, is a huge threat for people that tell themselves they're superior and should be admired and adored. How dare anyone giggle about their grandiosity when it should be regarded with the utmost awe! Could it be that they aren't so superior after all?

I've noticed throughout my life that the more you react to people making fun of you, the more they'll do it. Where's the fun in poking the bear when the bear doesn't react? Non-reaction will eventually bore the bullies, and they will stop. My ginger friend hardly reacted to our ginger jokes. The jokes went on for a few years, but his non-reaction paid off eventually. Almost no one teases him anymore.

"If we make the use of revenge merely as a remedy, let us use it without anger, and not regard revenge as pleasant, but as useful: yet often it is better to pretend not to have received an injury than to avenge it."

~ Seneca, *On Anger*, Book II, XXXII
(translated by Aubrey Stewart, 1900)

There's a YouTuber I've been watching for a while. I can't remember how exactly I bumped into his channel, but this particular person is an interesting example of how not to be unoffendable. Let's call him Coach since he presents himself as a 'life coach.' The content of his daily shows, however, is anything but life coaching. It's mostly theatrics, calling out people he doesn't like and offering help to those that aren't really asking for it. Coach's behavior has attracted a lot of criticism over the years up to the point of becoming a running joke on YouTube.

Coach is a very profitable person to troll because it's so easy to get a reaction out of him before he expels you from his channel. His shows always include a live chat that anyone can join (unless you're banned). I've never seen one of his shows without someone trolling him in the chat. Sometimes it's another content creator that's associated with him. In other cases, these are anonymous trolls, whose nicknames alone already suggest that they're up to no good. These trolls often manage to trigger Coach within the first five minutes of his broadcast before he banishes them. It's not rare that he resorts to cursing because he's so agitated by what they say. Or he says: "I don't care what you think," in a way that clearly shows that he does. If you're a true troll and you've managed to provoke your target, does it really matter if you get banned? You've accomplished your goal by getting a reaction out of the target, so your actions can be seen as a *kamikaze* mission accomplished. Because Coach reacts so easily, he attracts a huge number of trolls. The only method that works for him is banning a troll immediately without even reacting to them because this would give the trolls practically zero gratification for their actions. If he would just stop being reactive and ignore the trolls, then he'd be able to do what he says he's on YouTube for, which is life coaching.

Ignoring insults comes in different variations.

In the information age, there's more communication than ever before. Email, WhatsApp and social media flood us with messages. At the same time, they're easier than ever to ignore. When I was a child, the only conventional forms of communication were either letters and telegrams or phone calls, apart from face-to-face. It's easy to ignore a letter and a telegram by not responding, but it isn't easy to ignore someone speaking on the phone or in real life. When we refuse to respond to a 'live' insult, we automatically show that the person said something that affected us. A mid way ploy is giving someone a death-stare. A death-stare doesn't involve any words, but the silence and body language speak volumes. Imagine you're in a group setting. All eyes are on you and the troll.

TROLL : How're you doing four eyes? (an insult directed at your glasses).

YOU : …(with a blank stare)

TROLL : What's wrong? Lost your tongue?

YOU : … (blank stare; people starting to chuckle and giggle)

TROLL : We know you can't see very well, but we didn't know you're deaf, too.

YOU : ... (gives the death-stare)

TROLL : Hee hee, just kidding... (gets the shivers)

A death-stare is hostile. The advantage is that this could intimidate the insulter. The disadvantage is that it shows that we are affected and that the insulter has the power to alter our mood state. Most people would be affected by any good eye-to-eye stare in silence. My ginger friend would also apply the stare technique when made fun of in group settings. This wasn't a death-stare. It was rather a playful, disapproving stare accompanied by a very subtle smile. It was the 'well, well, well' stare that showed disapproval of the insult combined with a sense of friendliness and amusement. It's how we'd approach a puppy that did something naughty – and who on earth could be insulted by a puppy? Here's how it goes:

ME : Hey, do you know why the ginger went to

South-Korea?

    FRIENDS : No?

    ME : To find Seoul!

    FRIENDS : (laughing)

    GINGER: … (gives me the 'well, well, well' stare)

    ME : (laughing like a ten-year-old boy)

I remember that such stares resonated with my inner, naughty boy, making me laugh about my own childish tricks. Suddenly, I was the object of ridicule and not my ginger friend. Again, he didn't come off as 'butt-hurt,' which implied that my joke didn't really affect him. It wasn't my intention to hurt him, anyway, because he's my friend. It was a playful way to engage with him and he handled it quite well.

Much of the time, the effectiveness of non-reaction depends on which form of communication is used. At the time when the popularity of online "just for fun" platform 9GAG was at its peak, we used these typical 9GAG-styled memes and altered them to tease each other in a Facebook chat group exclusively for

184

friends. Although my ginger friend used the stare as a reaction to 'live' insults in group settings, he flat out ignored the ginger jokes in the Facebook chat group. The ability to simply ignore digital communication is a blessing in disguise. Let's face it: why would we get upset by something that we can simply turn off?

Up till today, our ginger friend scarcely responds to messages on group chats. He's probably busy working on his career or spending time with his wife and son. Where's the fun in sending out memes in group chats when the target is hardly there to respond? So, I'd say that non-reaction is extremely effective for digital forms of communication. We aren't obliged to respond to anything. Some messages are of such importance that it's better to respond out of responsibility, but we aren't obliged to. In some cases, the law requires us to respond, which makes us obligated in a way, but we still have freedom of choice whether to react or not (we'll face the consequences afterward). So, why should we feel the need to respond to insults?

Self-deprecating humor

Although non-reaction can be effective against insults, it isn't always the most glamorous option in 'live' situations. If someone throws you an insult with great hostility, it might be better to just avoid and ignore that person. But when someone's making fun of you in a social setting, there might be better ways to deal with it. Deciding on the best way to react in a certain situation requires a sensitivity to the social dynamics at play. Is there a sense of hostility involved? Is the environment tight or relaxed? Is 'mockery' the normal way to communicate with each other in this company? Some groups of people rarely mock each other, while others don't do anything but. I've noticed that the less seriously you take yourself, the easier it is to handle mockery.

When I traveled to Indonesia it always struck me how 'not-seriously' people tend to take themselves, especially the poorer people. They ridicule each other all the time and seem to be minimally affected by it. My ex-girlfriend who's of Indonesian descent and lived there till the age of fourteen noticed a difference between bullying in Indonesia and bullying in the Netherlands. According to her, people in Indonesia tend to tease each other a lot in a subtle playful manner, while the Dutch are more in-your-face and blunt in their comments. On the one hand, we cannot deny that more extreme cases of bullying are prevalent in Indonesia, like racial slurs and physical violence. But, still, there seems a less serious vibe overall among Indonesians in comparison to the Dutch, which makes the Indonesians a bit more pliable and playful in regards to teasing. I've noticed this with myself as well. When I'm serious and uptight, I'm more likely to get triggered by insults. Being serious and uptight is a consequence of telling myself certain stories, like "I'm a very important person" or "I must be taken seriously to reach a specific goal." The more I hold on to these stories, the stronger the ego becomes and the quicker I react when the ego is attacked. But when I'm in a more loose, relaxed and "I don't really have a story" mode, I don't get triggered so easily. Why should I? When I'm nothing, nothing can threaten me.

When we are in a more loose state, we can engage in playful ways to deal with insults. A great way to do this is by using humor, self-deprecating humor, in particular. My former coworker Carl I've told you about is a master at this. Carl is brown-haired, blue-eyed half Dutch and half Jordanian. At some point a few other coworkers and I starting teasing him about his Jordanian heritage, calling him 'Hashemite' and 'Arabi.' Instead of getting angry, he simply started to imitate Arabic people himself, whenever we teased him. This not only was very funny; it also showed that he wasn't triggered at all by the nicknames we threw at him.

The way he handled these insults really resonated with my own history of being made fun of because of my Middle Eastern looks. I started to understand that 'joining the play' is a very effective method of handling these forms of teasing. These days, when someone mocks me by saying that I look like a Moroccan, I just start talking like a Moroccan. Or, when someone makes fun of my Indonesian descent, I just do an imitation of a typical person from the Dutch-Indies. In most, if not all cases, doing this has a positive effect. I believe that the reason for this method's success is that it shows people that you're a fun person, who doesn't take himself or herself so seriously. Even Stoic philosopher Epictetus used humor when confronted with insults, saying: "If you hear that someone is speaking ill of you, instead of trying to defend yourself you should say: 'He obviously does not know me very well since there are so many other faults he could have mentioned.'

Meeting with violence

The Bible says that, if someone strikes you on one cheek, you should turn to him the other also (Luke 6:29). Does that mean that we should tolerate physical abuse? No, it doesn't. It means that we should answer an insult with an invitation to be insulted even more. American theologian John Schoenheit said that "In the Biblical culture, striking someone on the cheek was an insult." Back in the days of Jesus Christ, slapping someone on the right cheek in the presence of others was a method of public shaming. This way of shaming is still alive today; assuming that the majority of people use the right hand to perform the slapping, we can only slap the left cheek in a backhanded fashion. A backhanded slap isn't about inflicting damage. It's about humiliation.

Jesus Christ says that we shouldn't retaliate against this form of humiliation. There's a distinction between physical violence and insults. Physical violence harms the body. Insults, however, only harm us when we let them. Are we really going to run the risk of getting our lives ruined because someone calls us a name? "You're walking down the street and somebody calls you a name. You're gonna walk across the street, get into a fistfight, get thrown in jail, get your whole life derailed, just because someone called you a name?" says Schoenheit. Getting triggered by an insult is one thing; using violence to respond to an insult is even more stupid. Unfortunately, violence often begins with insults. I've already given the example of how insulting one's mother can lead to murder. Another recurring dynamic is soccer supporters that always begin by insulting each other before they resort to physical violence, resulting in people getting hurt, getting arrested or even killed.

I remember getting into a drunken brawl a few years ago. This started with a slew of words until the guy took a step back and punched me in the face. I fell backward in a Ted Mosby kind of fashion. I was so intoxicated that I hardly felt the punch and wasn't even aware that the bouncer immediately threw my opponent out of the bar. The next morning I woke up with swollen lips, actually feeling the punch. When the wound was healed, I forgot about it. Weeks later I met my cousin who had witnessed the punch and told me that when he sees the guy he'll whoop his ass. What baffled me is that I truly didn't experience any kind of resentment towards that guy. For me, the incident was simply passing out by intoxication combined with a violent bar scene. Who cares? Sure, I should have defended myself in that moment, but I don't see this incident as a reason for revenge. In the grand scheme of things, this fight was just a small thing that isn't worth acting upon, like a barking dog.

In his essay *On Anger*, Seneca tells us about roman senator Cato who was struck in the public baths. When the fight was over he refused to take an apology and said: "I do not remember being struck."

"It is the part of a great mind to despise wrongs done to it; the most contemptuous form of revenge is not to deem one's adversary worth taking vengeance upon. Many have taken small injuries much more seriously to heart than they need, by revenging them: that man is great and noble who like a large wild animal hears unmoved the tiny curs that bark at him."

~ Seneca, *On Anger*, Book II, XXXII
(translated by Aubrey Stewart, 1900)

While this book offers ways to minimize the harmful effects of an insult, being attacked physically is of a different order. If you're physically threatened, being unoffendable won't protect you against violence. You either run away, take the beating or defend yourself. How we approach physical violence really depends on the situation. Knowing that insults often lead to violence, non-reaction to insults often works wonders in regards to prevention. Potentially hostile situations can then be de-escalated.

Many martial arts experts value the application of non-violence in hostile situations. There's a famous story told from the perspective of a well trained, young

Aikido practitioner named Terry Dobson about a raging drunk that entered a train and began harassing passengers. Dobson, who lived in Japan at the time, saw the drunk as an opportunity to test his martial arts abilities. His master, however, forbade him to fight. "Aikido is the art of reconciliation," he said. "In Aikido, we study how to resolve conflict. Not how to start it." Nevertheless, Terry couldn't restrain himself and decided to kick the drunk's ass. Just before a physical fight broke out, Terry and the drunk were interrupted by an old man. This man managed to calm down the drunk with words of kindness and compassion. "What I had just witnessed was true Aikido in combat. The essence of it was love, as the founder had always said," said Terry afterward.

Chapter 9 – Living Life to the Fullest

Being unoffendable is a way to present ourselves in the world. It's an attitude of someone that doesn't get unnerved by all manner of things, focuses on the things that truly matter, bravely pursues their goals and ideals and doesn't mind sometimes being vulnerable. All this in order to grow. Someone who's unoffendable takes life as it comes and makes the best out of it, no matter what. In this closing chapter, I want to lay the final foundation for becoming unoffendable, and explain how we can harness this power to live well.

Being unoffendable doesn't mean being a coward. Rather, it's the art of not sweating the small stuff to achieve the great. No matter if we talk about Epictetus, Seneca, Marcus Aurelius or the Buddha, all were men of virtue. All learned to care less about the things that aren't important so they could achieve the great. Because our ginger friend doesn't give a damn about our ginger jokes, he saves energy for excelling in his work. Because our life coach has literally wasted years of his life on fighting trolls on his YouTube channel, he has yet to achieve what he set out to do.

Becoming braver

The Stoics consider cowardice a vice. The opposite of cowardice is courage. It's not uncommon that people mask their cowardice with virtuous acts. Masking fear with virtue is avoiding things we're afraid of, while making this seem an act we do out of goodness. Being unoffendable doesn't mean that we wear this mask. Our stance doesn't come from a place of fear but from a place of bravery. It's brave to act regardless of the opinions of others. It's brave to keep going forward no matter what people say. But when someone truly harasses us or attacks us physically – especially when our lives are in danger – it isn't virtuous to let ourselves be abused. In that case, it's better to address it or remove ourselves from the scene. Even walking away takes courage. How many people are afraid to walk away from an abusive relationship because they fear the unknown? How many people remain friends with toxic people because they're afraid of being alone?

Let me give you some examples of how being

195

unoffendable will lead to courage rather than cowardice. Imagine that you're part of a cult. After living a few years in that cult, you begin to see more and more of how destructive that life is. Like many cults, the one you're in is characterized by control in the form of shaming and ridicule. This means that, when you say something that goes against the cult's ideology, other cult members shame you – let alone if you decide to leave it. When you're unoffendable, you'll more likely have the courage to leave that stronghold because you don't really care what others think anyway. Also, you won't go through a lot of difficulty of confessing to your family and (old) friends that you were deceived and how stupid it was to enter it in the first place. You won't be afraid of their reactions. This makes it a lot easier to be vulnerable as well, which I'll talk about in a bit.

The Stoics value justice. In fact, justice is one of their four cardinal virtues. How can we pursue justice without courage? And how can we be courageous enough to pursue justice if we're slaves to other people's opinions? When an authority figure says something unreasonable, many people stay silent under the guise of 'politeness,' even when they know it's better to speak up. By doing this, they make way for injustices to spread freely and without resistance. In reality, they are afraid. And they're so ashamed about it that they rather hide their fears behind the curtain of virtue. I have lost count of the times I stayed silent when it was better to speak, or acted 'nice' instead of 'just.' Even though I knew that assertiveness was something I had to work on (and still do for the greater part), I have always been afraid to show the world my weaknesses. Sadly enough, my concern for other people's opinions was holding me back from doing the right thing. There is wisdom in King Solomon's words:

"To everything there is a season,
A time for every purpose under heaven ...
A time to keep silence,
And a time to speak ..."

~ Ecclesiastes 3:1,7

The true fighters for justice don't let the judgments of others stop them. They demonstrate that they aren't afraid to speak up. One of these people is

Dr. Jordan Peterson. Not everyone agrees with his views, and I don't support everything he says. Nevertheless, we cannot deny that he has risked his career by speaking out about many controversial topics concerning politics and religion. During the Manning Conference in 2007, he said something profound:

"Don't underestimate the power of truth. There's nothing more powerful. Now, in order to speak what you regard as the truth, you have to let go of the outcome. You have to think: okay I'm going to say what I think, stupid as I am, biased as I am, ignorant as I am, I'm going to state what I think as clearly as I can, and I'm going to live with the consequences no matter what they are."

~ Dr. Jordan Peterson, *Manning Conference* (2007)

Peterson pointed out that we should do the right thing regardless of the outcome. Although he encourages us to not let the fear of a possible negative outcome stop us, the Stoics go a step further saying that we should actually love the outcome. Although I've already discussed *amor fati* in previous chapters, I think it's an essential element in becoming more courageous.

Personally, I've let the fear of fate prevent me from taking action on many occasions. I'd rather avoid friends when I had a problem with them. I'd rather walk away from relationships than face my fear of commitment. As I admitted in the previous chapter, I lacked the courage to address bullies in high school. When I look back, I've never truly and completely spoken my mind before the biggest villain in my life: my dad. I've always wanted to be 'nice' and polite, which, in reality, was a way of masking my fear of confrontation. A fear of confrontation is basically a fear of being hurt. In most cases this hurt is mental, but sometimes it's physical. From the outside, my 'niceness' gave me a very calm, friendly exterior. But underneath I was often boiling. That's why I sometimes exploded after avoiding confrontation for a long time, which sometimes caused untold damage. After all: the ultimate goal of the Stoics isn't the avoidance of life. Quite the opposite: it's living a life that flourishes.

A courageous person doesn't necessarily feel less fearful than a coward. It's just that he doesn't let this fear hold him back. I discovered this quite late in life after a conversation I had with my stepfather about fear. A week earlier, I found myself in the same situation as the famous Terry Dobson. An aggressive, drunk guy had entered the train and started harassing people. However, instead of a fight response, I experienced a flight response. As I began fighting that fear, it only became stronger. Nevertheless, I called the ticket inspector and backed him up when he threw the drunk out of the train. After the incident, I hated myself for being such a coward for being fearful in that situation. Ideally, it should have been I that fearlessly kicked the guy out of the train like Superman and become the hero of the day.

In reality, I'm not a hero at all. I've always been quite anxious. Since childhood, my father has shamed me for being afraid. He has always claimed that he is fearless and that fear is wrong. That's why I've always felt ashamed of being fearful. My stepfather, on the other hand, quite recently explained to me that fear is normal and that he would also have experienced fear in the same situation. The trick is acting despite the fear. And that's what courage is. Building courage isn't about becoming less fearful. It's about becoming braver. Paradoxically, by repeatedly acting despite the fear, chances are that the fear itself reduces overtime.

Thrive

This may sound weird, but I kind of look up to the outcasts of society, even though I don't agree with them or support their actions. For example, Dutch politician Geert Wilders from the Dutch Freedom Party (PVV) is one of the most criticized and ridiculed people in the Netherlands. Not only because of his anti-Islam agenda and controversial statements, but also because of his dyed blonde hair. Despite insults, death threats and the need for 24/7 security, he keeps on doing his thing. Even the 'life coach' I told you about gains at least a modicum of my respect because, despite all the dislikes below his videos as well as trolls, parodies, satire and downright hateful comments, he just keeps putting himself out there.

Another example of this almost indestructible outcast is David Goggins whom I told you about earlier. Goggins let his past of being bullied fuel him to achieve incredible things. On the YouTube show

Impact Theory by Tom Bilyeu, he gave this very simple yet powerful advice on how to start the journey to greatness:

"If you can for, the rest of your life, live inside of yourself, stop listening to people that call you fat, gay, transexual, nigger, everything that makes no sense, all these people that put insecurities on you, you gotta flush it out."

~ David Goggins, *Impact Theory* / Tom Bilyeu (2018)

I'd summarize the message of this quote as 'becoming unoffendable.' Getting to the point where he was not afraid to face the thing on the other side of the door that wants to attack you, made him happy. Needless to say, to get there, David had to face his fears. He had to be courageous to be, as he claims, "the happiest man in the world." Hence, the Stoics see courage as a moral virtue, and moral virtue leads to *eudaimonia* – happiness.

An important side note is that, according to the Stoics, courage should be used to achieve something good that benefits humanity. It stands for virtue. Adolf Hitler was courageous to build up the Third Reich but that doesn't mean he did the right thing. I mean: can we see the genocide of millions of Jews as moral? Surely not. Also, courage shouldn't be a breeding ground for foolishness either. Foolishness is a Stoic vice. Many overly courageous people easily turn into blithering idiots that sacrifice themselves for the interests of the hidden puppet masters pulling the strings, or completely ruin their reputation by doing stupid things in the name of bravery. I've once reported on a demonstration of 'radical Muslims' in Jakarta. After some research I discovered that many of these people come from the rural areas and get paid a few shekels to go to the capital and yell extremist slogans, carry hateful banners and burn some flags. Moreover, the majority of them barely know what they're doing; yet they lend themselves to being filmed and photographed by the media. These are useful idiots, ignorantly sacrificing themselves for the benefit of (often invisible) the puppet masters.

Depending on the situation and your goal, it's better to play it smart sometimes. I could show my face in my YouTube videos, for example. Even though this is a courageous act, it also has a downside in that my face will be all over the internet: people may start to recognize me on the streets and the attention might actually obstruct me from doing my thing. Because I value my privacy and the tranquility that comes with that, it would be a foolish decision to show my face in my videos. Maybe that will change someday. Who knows!

In Buddhism, courage is highly valued as a necessity for reaching Buddhahood. In the thirteenth century, the Japanese Buddhist priest Nichiren wrote a letter to his brother Hyōe no Sakan Munenaga in which he offers advice on how to walk the Buddhist path during the age of moral decline.

"It is lack of courage that prevents one from attaining Buddhahood, although one may have professed faith in the Lotus Sutra many times since innumerable kalpas ago."

~ Nichiren, *The Three Obstacles and Four Devils*

Earlier in the book, I've already told you about the Buddha's path to enlightenment. To reach this path he did a series of controversial things, choosing a different path than his father laid out for him and leaving the security and comforts of the palace, including his wife and children. Even though some may see the latter as cowardly, it must have taken great courage to override his attachments to his loved ones to pursue something that, eventually, would change and benefit humanity to this day. Pursuing virtue with courage takes sacrifice. One sacrifices 'lesser' things like reputation, material possessions and relationships with people, to attain a higher goal.

Courage doesn't always have to be a heroic act. It's an attitude, a way of life. In Stoicism, courage is subdivided into endurance, high-mindedness, confidence, industriousness, and cheerfulness. Thus, there's more to courage than acting like a superhero, and it could very well be acts of consistency and persistence in doing morally right things. That's why walking a certain spiritual path can be a very courageous thing to do.

In the Indian religions, there's a concept called *Brahmacharya*, which is a way of life that includes the voluntary restraint of certain pleasures like sex and food. The self-restraint that's part of this lifestyle is regarded as a virtue, which paves the way to spiritual development. It isn't easy to abstain from pleasure, especially when those all around you are having fun indulging. Quitting alcohol, for example, is so difficult in the West because it's a socially accepted drug and the only drug in the world for which its rejection demands an explanation. Non-drinkers face resistance, criticism and even ridicule, even though I view abstaining from toxic and mind-altering substances as a good thing. Nevertheless, the majority of Westerners love drinking, see drinking as part of life and go to great lengths to defend their habit of consuming poison. Thus, the simple act of abstaining from things consistently for the sake of a better life can very well be an act of courage. All in all, being unoffendable is a stepping stone to becoming braver because we care less about what others think. This makes it easier to speak up during a meeting at work, express unpopular opinions and become as tough as David Goggins, or address a raging drunk peaceably like Terry Dobson. It also includes pursuing spirituality.

Proving myself wrong

When I finished a 10-mile race in 2018 I finally proved

myself wrong. In my youth, I was terrible at sports, apart from gymnastics, which I pursued for a few years. I sucked good at soccer and my stamina was far below average. I've inherited short, sturdy legs from my mother's family. They're strong and muscular but not really suited for running long distance. I remember that the fast kids would pass me twice when we did a Cooper test in high school on the athletics track. "Nope, running isn't for me," I always told myself.

Flash forward about twenty years. The Ten Miles is a yearly running event in my city. My youngest brother who served the military and fought in Afghanistan, ran the Ten Miles earlier despite the IED attack that caused permanent damage to his back and his brain. I really admired him for that, in fact, everyone who participated. I wished I could do that, too, but I thought: "I can never do that." Remembering my past experiences reinforced my self-doubt.

However, it all came to a head when at one point I decided that I wanted to do exactly this: run those Ten Miles. So, in 2017 I started training which was, overall, a dreadful and painful experience. A year later, I finished. It was exhilarating. Not many of my achievements matched the sense of fulfillment I had when I crossed that finish line. It's great to achieve something. It's even greater to achieve something that you thought you never could. My friend Barry happens to be a very well trained runner, who competed at a high level when he was in university. He said to me afterwards: "You ran with the speed of a snail. But you finished – and that's what counts."

Although my athletic achievements are peanuts compared to David Goggins, I can really relate to him when it comes to my youth. Like him, I was also a weak kid, facing racism and bullying, anxious and equipped with terribly low self-esteem. I looked bad, was teased because of my thin arms, was bad at sports and had even worse social skills. These experiences left a mark. But, when I was seventeen I decided to flip the script. Like me, Goggins first started out trying desperately to fit in because no one liked him. He developed many different identities for himself to try to fit in with different groups. I, too, remember desperately trying to make everyone like me. It was pathetic. Why was I doing it? Well, because I was so afraid of being ridiculed. But, you know what? Being ridiculed is part of life. A-holes and jerks are part of life. Avoiding them restricts our movement. Trying to make them like us is a waste of time. The only thing we can do is to grab life by the balls and thrive. To thrive, we have to be thick-skinned and ready to meet an army of trolls that try to trip us up at every turn. Many of these trolls are living in our memories of the past.

Another dragon to slay was school. Even though I obtained a bachelor's degree when I was 25 years old, I'd always been a terrible student. So bad, that my high school principal once suggested I just quit school. Also, the father of my former high school buddy told him that I would never make it in life, which kind of hurt. It confirmed my negative self-image. I internalized it and it became a model of laid-backness for the next few years. I was lazy, unmotivated, undisciplined, couldn't concentrate well, and left almost all the decisions for me to my father. Hence, I experienced these 'doomer phases' in my twenties because I wasn't really living. I was being lived. If you're living someone else's life (and many do) how can you ever be truly motivated?

I began college studying economics and

management, a subject my father had picked for me. I failed. After that, I made a leap to social studies. This wasn't really because I liked it but because my friend Hamid picked it, I just followed him. All in, it took me six years to graduate for my bachelor's degree instead of the usual four.

Rejection under my feet

But the final year changed something in me. To graduate, we had to form groups. Those that liked each other had formed groups themselves, which led to the best students forming groups together. The rejects, however, were dispersed over other groups. Among the rejects were the worst of the worst that no one wanted to work with. The school decided to put these people into one group and I was among them. And so was the ADHD guy I told you about earlier. So, there we were. Three guys and a girl. Everybody knew what was going on. We were a walking wall of shame. A particular young lady met us with contempt. The way she spoke to us, and the way she (apparently) talked behind our backs made it clear that she thought we were the pits.

Ironically, being put together because no one else wanted us fueled us to do something great. It motivated us. We started kicking ass. A year later we finalized our project scoring three nines (a ten being the highest grade possible). We literally had the best grades of all students. Why? Because, despite our infamy, we believed in ourselves, in each other and our project. After we received our grades, I asked the arrogant young lady about her grade: "A seven," she said irritated. I laughed and went straight to the pub with my awesome group members to celebrate our victory. This was really one of the best payback moments I'd ever experienced in my life.

The success continued the year after when my passion for video drove me to travel to Indonesia to shoot a documentary that was screened in one of my city's film theaters. This led to quite an amount of media attention. Achieving this, taught me two very important life lessons that I carry around to this day: (1) You can do way more than you think. (2) Great things always start with just a simple idea. It hurts me sometimes to see so many people with fantastic ideas and talents but fail to act on them. Why do they choose

211

the safe route rather than take the risks? Mostly, it's because they are afraid of failure. Not just the failure itself, but because of what other people would think and say about them. If you have an idea and believe in it: just... freaking... do it. There's always a legion of trolls on the sidelines telling you not to. There's always this friend or family member that tells you you're stupid. Unless they have something valuable to say, I'd say: ignore them. Life is ticking away second after second. The moment to escape mediocrity is now. If you stop being a slave to the opinions of others, it doesn't matter if you fail. Even if you do, you just shrug it off and start again, hopefully, smarter, wiser and more experienced.

The birth of Einzelgänger

With a high always comes a low. As the Stoics repeatedly point out, external things are unreliable and impermanent. Success comes and goes. And when we tie our happiness to these external factors, we set ourselves up for a rollercoaster ride. But, you know, that doesn't mean that we shouldn't pursue something.

212

It's just a matter of what we pursue. Little did I know that the way I had learned to live life was getting me nowhere and that someday, I'd throw in the towel and turn inwards. What I had done so far brought me a few material accomplishments, yes, but when it came to happiness and inner peace I was a complete wreck. I self-medicated with alcohol just to get through bouts of anxiety.

The period that followed after two successful years of accomplishment was one of stagnation. Directly after my graduation, I worked in that warehouse for a year. During that time I ended a six-year relationship. It was painful. Despite the severe financial crisis we were in, I found a job at a bank after two months of unemployment. This is the semi-student job where I met Barry, Carl, my ginger friend, and other guys I've talked about. From that point on a new 'bloomer' phase began.

In regards to women, I had no self-esteem. In me was a deeply ingrained storyteller who told me that I sucked at attracting women. My friends were basically all couples, doing 'couples things' and I felt isolated in these friendships. Gradually, I found new

213

social circles, new friendships and created opportunities to go out and meet women. Even though this went together with going to bars, heavy drinking and using recreational party drugs, I had the time of my life. Becoming better with women is a painful process during which we can expect rejection and even being insulted by the opposite sex. But, after approaching more and more women, I cared less about what they thought and that's when I started making progress. Check.

Alongside my affairs with the opposite sex, I was slaying yet another dragon. I have to thank my father, the villain, for this one, though. One day in the pub he told me that I was stagnating. He suggested that I pick a new challenge in the form of a master's degree and promised that he'd support me. After making a documentary about Islam, I developed a greater interest in religion and spirituality, so I chose to study religion and ritual. Although some would argue this is just another worthless degree, it is something that I am highly interested in. This was the first time in my life I truly studied. Despite all my binge drinking, chasing women, rock-star-like lifestyle, I graduated two years later and without overtime, with a 7.5. I went from being a terrible student that was told to give up school to obtaining a master's degree. Check.

However, the years that followed my graduation were the most difficult and darkest years of my life. I drank too much, I had terrible anxiety, I was depressed. A family drama concerning my father had erupted, which continues to this day. I've suffered immensely because of it. At one point my depression was so deep that I wanted to kill myself. At that time I still worked at the bank, sometimes staring out of the window from the sixth floor, thinking about jumping. And when I walked back into my department, there was this annoying coworker singing: "shni-shna-snatsy snatsy-snatsy-snats."

After my relationship of two years ended, I decided to stay single for a long, long time. I realized that the only way to get out of this misery was sitting by myself and turning within. I had to let go of societal expectations and just be me. This process took a few years. Philosophy began to play a major role in that period. In fact, I went on a binge.

Since late 2016 I've been living a solitary life.

It may be temporary; it may be not. During my solitary life, I've been able to free myself from resentment towards many things: family, old friends, women and, well, society in general. I had to shake off a lot of trolling to stick with this 'loner lifestyle.' People started to comment on the fact that I have been single for such a long time, and I should find a girlfriend. And, when I decided to stop drinking (at least for a prolonged period) people criticized me for being an ascetic. Nevertheless, I believe that this period of introspection was necessary for my personal growth. Yes, I lost friends and my party days are long gone. But now I'm not living for others anymore. Paradoxically, now I'm indeed truer to myself, better able to contribute to the world. By caring less I learned to care more about humanity (myself included) and the things I deem truly important.

In December 2018 I started the YouTube channel *Einzelgänger* and I'm very happy with the experience so far. When I started this, several people predicted this would not work out well and I'd be better off working a nine-to-five job. Yes, it's risky. But "You gotta risk it to get the biscuit" an old party buddy of mine used to say. Needless to say, I'm happy that I ignored the critics and pushed through. It was worth it. Einzelgänger gives my life meaning and I feel I've got something to share to the world.

I still have many hurdles to jump, fears to conquer and finish lines to cross. Now that I've dropped the drinking habit, I'm basically reinventing my social skills. It's become very clear to me that shyness and social anxiety are the main reason I drank in the first place. And, as I finalize this book, I'm about to go on a journey abroad to throw myself out there again, face my fears, find inspiration and shoot some decent footage for my channel.

The sun is shining. It's a beautiful day. Let's cherish the time we have by caring less about the things that don't matter so we can pursue the things that do. It doesn't matter whether we seek to achieve spiritual enlightenment, travel the world, make a fortune, start a family, or perhaps just ask for help. *Memento mori.* The time is ticking, my friends.

End quote,

Einzelgänger

91763380R00132